"Barbara is well-known in the e̶n̶g̶ ... ... as a capable leader and for her ability to organize and pilot high-functioning teams. She is the true epitome of a valued servant leader."
—*Van Collins, President and CEO, American Council of Engineering Companies (ACEC) Washington*

"It is known that the quality of one's leadership is most clearly revealed in the crucible of an organization's crises. Barbara's vital walk with Christ and her experience in diverse leadership roles, including during profound crises, positions her well to offer us vital leadership insight and wisdom."
—*Rev. Greg Yee, Pacific Northwest Conference Superintendent, Evangelical Covenant Church*

"Barbara has a vast number of credentials and many years of experience, but what makes people follow her is her compassion, her dedication to inclusion, and her light that shines out from within. She is an inspiration to me!"
—*Heather Marx, Director of Downtown Mobility, City of Seattle, WA*

"I've known Barbara as a mentor, a peer, and friend for many years and I've always admired her intelligence and quick wit, her sharp problem-solving skills, and most of all, her ability to balance life and work seamlessly. She taught me early in my career that it's ok to be a strong, successful leader at work, while at the same time putting family first. It has been an honor and absolute pleasure working with Barbara over the years, and I can't wait to read this book!"
—*Angie Brady, Director of Waterfront Seattle, City of Seattle, WA*

"Many of us wish to be effective leaders throughout our entire life. Barb Moffat's use of Nehemiah stretches the reader to believe that each one can become the leader that God is asking for us to be... women and men of humble service with a mark on our lives to lead others. Barb thoughtfully brings us to the place of preparation for God speaking to us as He did to Nehemiah. Go and lead!"

—*Keith Hamilton, President, Alaska Christian College, Seward, AK*

"Barbara was our Church Chair while our congregation was going through some very difficult times. Her calm, decisive, and steady leadership was key in helping us stay on track, grieve, begin to heal, and move forward during pastoral transitions. As her successor as Chair, I am immensely grateful for her and her wisdom in leading our church to a healthier place and appreciate her insights from the book of Nehemiah that I've seen lived out in her leadership."

—*Rev. Merrie S. Carson, DMin, CSD*

Awaken the Leader Within You

Journey through Nehemiah to Expand your
Perception of Who a Leader Is

Barbara Ann Moffat

RIVER BIRCH PRESS

Daphne, Alabama

ISBN 978-1-956365-37-5 (print)
ISBN 978-1-956365-38-2 (e-book)

For Worldwide Distribution
Printed in the U.S.A.

River Birch Press
P.O. Box 868, Daphne, AL 36526

For leaders and those who are not yet
aware they are leaders

A leader is one who influences a specific
group of people to move in a God-given direction.
—J. Robert Clinton

Table of Contents

Acknowledgments

The author would like to thank...

...Sherri Goodwin, friend, who freely gave of her time to proof-read the raw manuscript...

...Keith Carroll, literary agent, who saw the potential of an unproven writer...

...Ethan Moffat, son, who unwittingly became my target audience...

...Deborah Moffat, daughter, who encouraged me to continue...

...James Moffat, husband, who believed in me throughout...

And most importantly,

...The Lord God, who was with me and directed this writing.

Preface

Several years ago, I prepared a devotion for a church leadership retreat. I wanted to shift our focus from upcoming agendas and committee reports to how we could better allow God to work through us in our current leadership positions. The devotion was intended to center our minds around the idea that our leadership team needed to follow Jesus—not just an itinerary.

With this being my first devotion, I honestly did not know how to start. Through a series of events, I began reading the book of Nehemiah, and I could not stop reading. Mesmerized, I read through the entire book in one sitting. I read it repeatedly, carefully seeking to hear what God was saying in each chapter of the book. I was amazed how God transformed me and my ideas of leadership through these multiple readings.

I realized that the leadership provided by Nehemiah was not simply the top-down hierarchical leadership we see in many organizations today. Instead, Nehemiah poured his leadership skills into the lives of those around him. Everyone was called to embrace Nehemiah's leadership methods regardless of societal position. He taught a leadership that was for everyone.

God showed me specific leadership themes in each chapter, giving me the thoughts and words to make them alive and relevant today. God took me on an exciting journey from believing that leadership skills were only for a select few to seeing how each of us is a leader in our own right, regardless of where or who we are!

If we hold to the view that only certain people are called to leadership, we will miss what God has planned for us individually. Through the book of Nehemiah, I learned that God wants each of us to consider ourselves leaders, exactly where He has placed us.

As you begin to live into the leadership concepts in this book, I hope the Word of God and the ideas He shared with me will also come alive for you. May you be blessed to see God working more fully in your life as you step further into your role as a leader.

Introduction

Why should you read this book? What makes it different from other leadership resources? As I began to study Nehemiah, an idea formed that I had never considered before. Even though I have been in leadership for many years, it surprised me. I became more and more excited as I pondered the central question, "Who is a leader?"

Simply put, this book is explicitly written for you. Even more remarkably, it is written for you regardless of whether you currently consider yourself a leader or someone called to leadership.

I believe that we must completely reframe our definition of a leader if we are to lead as God intends. I was amazed to see God transform my previous leadership ideas by enlarging my perception of that term.

In God's eyes, leadership is not about title or position but about recognizing that you are already in a leadership role, regardless of whether you are a pastor, deacon, CEO, teacher, housewife, mail clerk, janitor, or machinist. Incredibly, beyond all logic, I understood that God already sees us as a leader!

The leadership concepts in this book can be embraced by anyone willing to accept that leadership is not for a select few individuals but for anyone willing to grow. Our position or title is essential only to the extent that it helps us recognize how our unique skills complement the work others are called to do.

No one is more significant than anyone else; everyone is equally and vitally important for the body to function. We each have a role to play. I had to laugh at myself when I finally understood how to apply this simple truth to the context of leadership.

Once when my children were young, we went on a grueling all-day hike to a pristine mountain lake. It was a hot summer day, and we did not bring enough water. Multiple times (particularly when scrambling across sections of loose shale), our children asked to turn around. It was challenging, but we finally made it to the lake, ate lunch, and went back down the mountain.

Several months later, when speaking about this trip with an avid hiker, we received advice I have never forgotten: a hike should never be about the destination but the journey. To build a love of hiking into our kids, we needed to let go of getting there and enjoy the trail along the way.

As I have journeyed into leadership, I have learned to stop and look along the way. No solitary secret will instantly make you a leader. Instead, if we can agree that anyone in any walk of life is already a leader, then our pathway together is to simply develop that which is already inside of us.

The answer to why you should read this book is simple: this book will help you live more fully who you already are. Embracing and acting upon the leadership concepts in this book will empower you to become the leader God intends you to be while living and serving Him exactly where you are.

I'm excited to share these concepts with you. They will help you handle issues you encounter every day and allow you to become someone others want to emulate as they see your emerging leadership skills. I encourage you to read through the corresponding chapter in Nehemiah at the start of each chapter in this book to breathe life into each concept we explore. Study Questions appear in the Appendix for those wishing to dig more deeply into the ideas in each chapter.

This book covers three primary areas of leadership: situational, relational, and spiritual. Each includes specific principles that, when woven together, create a framework for expanding the range of your leadership skills from wherever you currently find yourself.

• **Situational Leadership** deals with leading through varying circumstances, whether moments of crisis, disaster, or joy. This is a leadership that honors God and entices others to follow even during daily, hectic life. As we encounter unique situations, these leadership concepts remain constant and universally applicable, becoming our go-to response when needed at a moment's notice.

• **Relational Leadership** covers the nitty-gritty leadership needed when dealing with others, whether they be hostile or friendly. Recognizing that we deal with all types of people daily, we need to hone our ability to understand the drivers behind others' actions. Relational leadership concepts can be utilized in our interactions with others in a way that brings God glory.

• **Spiritual Leadership** cannot simply be relegated to those in designated positions of authority. Each of us is called to develop the spiritual leadership skills needed to make a difference in someone else's life by showing them how to become more like Jesus. The skills we learn must become so ingrained that those we lead will be encouraged to follow our example.

The book of Nehemiah tells how God worked through Nehemiah to train up the next generation of leaders and how Nehemiah's reliance on God created a leadership model we can emulate today. Working together, each concept on this pathway will become a building block, allowing you to grow into a new understanding of leadership. I am excited to begin this journey with you as together we unfold the truth of your unique role as a leader.

ᑫ 1 ᑭ

Respond to Crisis

Now it came about when I heard these words, I sat down and wept and mourned for days; and I was fasting and praying before the God of heaven (Neh. 1:4).

WHY DO BAD THINGS HAPPEN to good people? This question has no ready answer. Bad things happen to everyone; it is a matter of *when* not *if*. At some point, you will be the recipient of unwelcome news. It may be a natural disaster, school shooting, or terrorist attack. It may be news about the death of a friend or loved one. It may be a cancer diagnosis, car accident, job loss, or unexpected alienation. There may be a social justice issue you are passionate about that seems insurmountable. Regardless of what it is, it may feel as though the entire world is caving in on you when you hear the news.

Your response will differ significantly depending on your proximity to the event or relationship with the person involved. Each situation will not only test your core beliefs but reveal the depth of those beliefs. Spoken or not, what you genuinely believe about God will rise to the surface. The good news is that you can learn to respond in a way that honors God.

The book of Nehemiah opens with the advent of bad news.

Nehemiah lives in the Babylonian capital of Susa, about 900 miles from Jerusalem. During a visit from his brother and some friends, he receives some disturbing news.

The Jewish people who have returned to Jerusalem after more than seventy years of exile in Babylon have found that they are in grave danger. During their captivity, the walls around the city of Jerusalem were destroyed. They have returned to a homeland without protection against anyone who might choose to attack.

The first chapter of Nehemiah tells us that Nehemiah has a position of prominence in King Artaxerxes' court. We do not know his family situation other than that he has received a visit from his brother. Was he open and receptive to these men? Was he excited by the prospect of a visit from his brother?

As we hear the news, we realize they are there for more than just a social visit. When Nehemiah asks this group of men about the exiles and Jerusalem, they give him specific intel about the destruction they have encountered. With Nehemiah's high position in court, they are likely not just giving him the news but have high expectations that he will also do something about it.

Hearing bad news is never easy. However, when it is shared, you may feel you want or should be able to help. Nehemiah 1 identifies three situational leadership concepts that will enable you to respond to any crisis in a way that honors God. Through this chapter we will explore the importance of a life of prayer.

Our first concept is to embrace a solid understanding of who we are. The second concept provides an immediate go-to response that will become second nature over time. The third concept teaches us to develop a healthy dependency upon God, leaning into and claiming His promises.

Core Identity

Our name is crucial to our identity. New parents often ponder over selecting their child's name, with much time spent looking through books on baby names or doing online research about the meaning of a name in its original language.

Why is a name so important? Either intentionally or unintentionally, people often grow into the meaning of their name. In the Bible, particularly in the Old Testament, names were carefully chosen based on their meaning. It was not uncommon for people to assume a new name or identity based on a situation they had encountered.

I grew up with two siblings who were given family middle names: my brother bears my mother's maiden name, and my sister carries my mother's first name. I always considered my middle name to be unimportant. Whenever I questioned my mother about her choice of my middle name, she would tell me that it was simply because she liked it.

This middle name, coupled with a first name that means "stranger or sojourner in a foreign land," only added to a feeling of not being as valued as my older siblings. This feeling grew to the point where I gladly changed my middle name to my maiden name when I was married. Aside from my birth certificate, all signs of "Ann" were erased from my life.

Several years after my parents died, I shared my feelings regarding my given middle name with my sister. She looked at me in confusion, not understanding. She knew something I did not. I had been given my middle name in honor of my mother's closest brother, Anders. Although my mother had told my sister this many times, she had not shared this with me.

It made a difference to know that I too had been given a

family name! Within a few months, I changed my middle name back to Ann. It is a name that has become precious to me and profoundly grounds me in my family roots.

———

In the very first sentence of Nehemiah, he identifies himself by his Jewish name. His self-introduction shows that regardless of the position to which he had risen in a foreign society, he had kept his core identity and heritage intact. He knew who he was.

Historians agree that Nehemiah grew up as a rising star in King Artaxerxes' court. Although King Nebuchadnezzar had attempted to integrate the Jews into the Chaldean culture, Nehemiah's self-identification by his Hebrew name tells us that the Jewish community retained its identity during captivity and that Nehemiah's personal identity was aligned with his faith in the God of Israel.

One can imagine the pressure he might have faced to conform to Babylonian culture, particularly when living in the king's court. Nevertheless, he maintained his Jewish identity and name, which means "YAHWEH comforts." Throughout each situation and crisis he encounters, Nehemiah's identity has a significant bearing on his response. Nehemiah's faith in God provides a foundation to which he returns repeatedly.

———

The ancient Greek aphorism of "know thyself" was a maxim weighty enough to be inscribed on the Temple of Apollo at Delphi. This saying encompasses not only an understanding of our strengths but also our weaknesses. It encourages us to understand ourselves well enough to know what values and beliefs motivate our reactions and responses, particularly in a crisis. When introducing ourselves, we often use descriptors that vary depending on who we meet. For personal introductions, after stating our name, we usually add descriptors such as how many children we have, what we do for work, or where we live. We may add our title, leadership role, or professional accomplishments at formal business events.

Descriptors separated from our core beliefs do not fully capture our identity. How often do you use the descriptor of "Christian" when describing yourself? Is it only in select situations?

In the business world, I have found that those in leadership are less likely to self-identify as Christians. We believe others expect us to be stoic, strong, decisive, action-oriented, and in control—and we may not think those traits are synonymous with being a Christian. This can happen not just in the business world but wherever you are in life. We play the part we assume that others want or expect of us and, over time, build a divide between our personal and public identities.

Mark 3:25 states, "If a house is divided against itself, that house will not be able to stand." The message is simple and straightforward: we cannot live two lives and expect God to honor our efforts. Before we can look at any other leadership concepts, we must clearly understand our identity—an identity rooted in Jesus.

Matthew 10:33 holds a sobering reminder: "But whoever shall deny Me before men, I will also deny him before My Father who is in heaven." Many years ago, I commented at work about going to church over the weekend. A surprised coworker stated, "Oh! I didn't know you were religious!" That cut me to the quick. My life looked so much like the lives of my non-Christian friends that no one at work knew I was a Christian. That left a deep mark on me, strengthening my resolve to bring my Christianity into visibility in every area of my life.

Is your identity rooted in Jesus Christ? Do you know who you are? Before reading any further, I encourage you to answer these questions. An identity founded upon Jesus is critical for allowing God to lead in and through you.

God does not only use those the world calls leaders. He wants to use each one of His people exactly where He has placed them. Knowing your identity is the first step toward vibrant leadership.

Go-To Response

How do you respond in a crisis? Are you calm and level-headed, or do your thoughts scatter, and you react in panic? Most of us have heard of the "fight-or-flight" response. Since the early 1900s, psychologists have known that our bodies have a physiological reaction to perceived harmful events, attacks, or threats to survival. As physical or mental events unfold, hormones are released into our system, preparing our body to stay and deal with the danger or run to safety.

Once when my infant son awoke from a nap, I went to open his door, and the door handle came off in my hands. As his screams escalated, so did my panic. My son was trapped! With spiraling fear, I could only think to call 9-1-1. The fire department responded with all units, including an ambulance, ladder truck, and fire chief. The neighbors must have thought the house was burning down. One of the firefighters went inside, calmly inserted a screwdriver into the doorknob, and the door swung open.

While I would like to say this was an isolated situation, I have learned that "flight" tends to be my typical response to a crisis. Although no consensus exists in the scientific community regarding whether humans can condition themselves to react to threats in a prescribed manner, I believe that learning a go-to spiritual response can help us respond to most situations. Regardless of our natural inclination, and with practice, that response can become our immediate reaction when a crisis strikes.

Crises almost always arise without notice. What happens when you learn of sexual immorality between close friends or become aware of financial improprieties or embezzlement by a family member? What do you do when gossip touches you, or a child is sexually abused by a trusted adult?

Extreme situations are not the only ones that may cause a flight response to be triggered. Sometimes the burden seems too great to handle, or it can be easier to defer to someone else. But fleeing a crisis could result in us missing the very opportunity God has intended for us to handle. While flight may be appropriate in some situations where physical safety may be at risk, most crises can benefit from an immediate learned spiritual response.

———

Nehemiah's reaction upon hearing bad news is an excellent place to start if we want to build our own solid go-to response. His immediate, pre-programmed response was connecting with God through deep grieving, prayer, fasting, and repentance. His reaction was measured and intentional, and he gave his full attention to bringing the situation to God.

First, we are told that Nehemiah sat down and wept and mourned for days. One may wonder why he was so grieved. Upon hearing the plight of his fellow citizens, the logical reaction might have been to want to fix the situation. Exactly what was he mourning? I believe he was grieving the brokenness between the people and God that fostered this crisis. We must learn the necessity of spending whatever time is needed to see the situation as God sees it, which may include time for grief.

As followers of Jesus, we need to respond as He would. Jesus said, "My soul is deeply grieved, to the point of death" (Matt. 26:38). He did not grieve for Himself, but because of the weight of sin He was to bear. When was the last time you went to your knees and wept for the brokenness of our world?

As we learn to lead through crises, we must take time to grieve over the sin that has erected a barrier between God and us in the situation. We must never be quick to jump to judgment or condemnation for others' actions or seek an immediate remedy.

Next, we see that mourning was not an end in itself. Nehemiah did not simply spend time mourning. His grief was coupled with fasting and prayer. Fasting clarified his thoughts and heart so he could hear how God wanted him to handle the situation more clearly.

If we are to lead through a crisis, we must not be quick to act on our own ideas. We can tend to rely on previous experience for the perfect solution to any situation. Contrast that with Nehemiah's approach: waiting on guidance from God before acting. As difficult as it may be, we must be willing to wait until we know how God wants us to move forward.

Finally, Nehemiah's prayers included a component of personal confession and repentance. Although he was living in luxury in the king's palace, his identity was so strongly tied to his fellow citizens that he included himself in his confession and repentance: "We have sinned against Thee, I and my father's house have sinned" (Neh. 1:6).

We must be willing to become intimately involved in any crisis we encounter. The troubles of others become our own. We must lead with repentance, taking ownership of acts against God, whether or not we are personally responsible for those acts. First Peter 2:9 states that God "has called you out of darkness into His marvelous light." Remembering the depth of the sin from which Jesus redeemed you will allow you to enter the brokenness of others with a humble spirit in genuine repentance.

For those who love Jesus, the immediate go-to response to any crisis begins with prayer, which may include grief, fasting, confession, and repentance. Turning to God first rather than trying to handle a situation on our own is crucial. Each time, it will become easier. Each instance will allow the learned response to become more and more ingrained until it eventually becomes our go-to response.

Foxhole Mentality

Most people are familiar with the saying, "There are no atheists in a foxhole." The premise behind this statement is that when people are at their lowest point, they will say anything to try to get out of it, including promising God pretty much anything. "Lord, if you help me just this once, I promise I will never (fill in the blank) again." This promise, typically given in earnest at the time, is rarely kept. Additionally, we often hope that God will turn a blind eye to how we got ourselves into the situation in the first place and jump to our aid.

It is good to remember that God can and will use anything to reach people— even foxholes. For some, it may take hitting that place of rock bottom before they will finally yield themselves to God. While God is indeed merciful and may choose to step in, it is also helpful to recall He is also just and will not necessarily shield us from the natural consequences of our actions and choices.

What does a foxhole mentality have to do with handling a crisis? It comes down to understanding that God longs for us to call out to Him in our need. Indeed, He sometimes allows us to reach those low places to get our attention.

God's ultimate desire is to restore our relationship with Him, whatever it takes. When a crisis hits, crying out to God is a sound and valid response wherever we are. A foxhole mentality is not just wishful thinking. We should never be afraid to call on God, foxhole or not!

The key is to have a sound knowledge of who God is and His promises so they can be claimed during a crisis. This takes it from a foxhole mentality of empty promises to a foxhole mentality of faithful expectation.

We see an example of calling on God with faithful expectation as we close out Chapter 1 of Nehemiah. Nehemiah has claimed his identity as an Israelite. He has fasted, confessed, and repented personally for the actions and inactions of his countrymen. He does not stop there.

He claims the promises God has made to the Israelites: God had warned His people that the unfaithful would be scattered, but He also promised to gather back together those who kept His commandments.

Nehemiah prays with a tone of expectation, not desperation. Rather than pleading or bargaining, he uses prayer to remind himself of what he already knows: God has been and always will be faithful to His people. Whether God's people are scattered or together, His covenant holds fast. Nehemiah's knowledge of God allowed him to pray in complete confidence that God would hear and respond.

A big question is do we need to remind God of His promises? When the world comes crashing down, it can feel as though God is not being quite as attentive as we might like. Maybe His response is not what we had hoped, or His timing seems to be off. We may question if He will rescue us.

The question at the start of this chapter still stands. Why do bad things happen to good people? Aren't you listening, God? We may often feel as if we need to remind God of what is going on in our life in case He has forgotten.

In 2001, Michael W. Smith wrote a popular worship song, "This is the Air I Breathe," which repeatedly states how desperate we are for Him. Singing these words is easy to do without considering the depth of healthy dependency represented.

We are encouraged to live in this same state, as spiritually reliant upon God in each moment as our bodies are reliant upon the air for each breath. This reliance is not one of vain hope but of faithful expectation that He will be with us in all circumstances.

The last component needed to be prepared to handle a crisis is simply relying on God and claiming His promises in all situations. We must learn what pleases Him and what causes Him pain. We must understand the tension between His mercy and justice. We must cultivate a relationship that causes us to desire to turn to Him first in any crisis. We need to rely upon Him desperately and then transparently model this sort of reliant dependency to others.

One thing that may be helpful to keep in mind is that foxholes were created to provide protection. If you ever find yourself in a desperate situation, remember that God may have placed that foxhole there to protect you.

In describing God to the Athenians, the apostle Paul

states, "that they should seek God, if perhaps they might grope for Him and find Him, though He is not far from each one of us." (Acts 17:27). Whether in a foxhole or not, reaching out to God is always the proper response to any crisis.

SUMMARY

Personal preparation is foundational to leading through a crisis and is the key to success. Feeling in control is easy when everything is going smoothly, but God often allows testing and trials to hone the tools we need to cope with a crisis. Each person is responsible for what they bring to the table.

First, know who you are. Your identity must be as a firm and unwavering follower of Jesus. Let that identity color everything you do. Secondly, choose the healthy go-to of prayer, fasting, confession, and repentance in any situation. Finally, cultivate a healthy dependency on God. Live each day in faithful expectation that He will meet your need.

These concepts can be embraced by anyone willing to lead through situations that arise in their life. Applying these situational leadership concepts will keep you from being overwhelmed when it feels like the world is caving in, and it will give you the confidence to step into the next lesson.

CONSIDER

As we close, identify one or two current (or previous) situations in your life that you consider a crisis. Practice applying the three situational leadership concepts explored in this chapter to this crisis. How is God working in this situation to bring you closer to Him?

PRAYER

Lord, help me embrace and claim my identity as a follower of Jesus. May my go-to response in any situation be to turn to You. In times of crisis, let me learn to grieve while turning to fasting and prayer. Let my heart be soft enough to see when I need to confess and repent, not just for my own sins but on behalf of others. Teach me to claim and speak the truth of Your past faithfulness as a precursor to Your continued action in the future. Amen.

⁓2⁓

Strategic Planning

And I arose in the night, I and a few men with me. I did not tell anyone what my God was putting into my mind to do (Neh. 2:12).

A CRISIS HAS ARISEN, or an opportunity may have presented itself. Even though you may have prepared for this moment, what are you to do? All eyes are on you. Others are expecting decisions and direction. Or so it may seem.

Some leaders will forge ahead, confident in their direction and actions. Some may pause, unsure where to begin, seeking input and advice before advancing. Others may be mired in procrastination and unable to move forward.

For those familiar with procrastination, although we fully intend to do what we have agreed to or know we must do, other priorities stall our progress. We may encounter difficulties that impede our ability to complete a specific task, or the job may simply be unpleasant. The longer a project languishes, the more stress builds until we are in full-blown procrastination mode.

Procrastination is simply delaying or avoiding something that one fully intends to do. Up to 20 percent of the American public procrastinates in one way or another. Some people make it into an art form by weaving an intricate web of delay or avoidance tactics. They have the techniques down pat!

Causes of procrastination vary depending on the job at hand. While the delay in tackling a specific task is sometimes unavoidable (or possibly even a better option), procrastination is rarely considered a desirable leadership trait. Most resources are devoted to helping people overcome any potential tendency toward procrastination, not the other way around.

———

Nehemiah 2 explores the next set of situational leadership skills that can be utilized in a crisis with a focus on a life of listening. These are skills that counter any proclivity for procrastination. Only after Nehemiah has prepared himself in Nehemiah 1 is he ready to move forward.

The end goal is not in question. Nehemiah plans to rebuild the wall around Jerusalem. After seeking God's input and direction, Nehemiah develops and begins to implement a solid strategic plan to accomplish this goal. Employing the leadership concepts in Nehemiah 2 to develop a strategic plan can eliminate procrastination.

The strategic plan has three elements. First, Nehemiah activates a strong base of support with those most influential to his success. Secondly, he performs an independent assessment of the situation to verify the accuracy of what has been reported. Finally, he issues a clear and compelling call to action, understanding that full engagement by every person at every level is the key to success.

Activating Support

Recently, my husband finished an extended streak of watching every *Lone Ranger* episode he could find. They reminded him of being a little boy, watching them on a small black-and-white TV set each week. He loved how the Lone Ranger always set things right. No matter the danger or situation, the Lone Ranger and his faithful sidekick, Tonto, always won—and the bad guys lost.

One night while discussing an episode, my husband mentioned that it was rare for the Lone Ranger to act alone. That was news to me! While he was, without doubt, the hero of the story, the Lone Ranger would alternately rely upon the sheriff, townspeople, or a nearby business owner. He activated support from those best positioned to provide the help he needed.

Deep within, many of us crave a chance to be a hero. While it may be admirable in a television series or movie, lone ranger decisions can be dangerous. Without question, sometimes a singular direction is needed; however, a collaborative approach often has a better result.

Situations can rapidly deteriorate when someone believes they can (or should) solve every issue by themselves. No one wants to be seen as weak or unsure of themselves. We must learn to understand the importance of collaboration and how to garner the type of support needed in each situation. Learning to leverage our influence is the critical component.

At the end of Nehemiah 1, we learn that Nehemiah is the cupbearer to King Artaxerxes. The cupbearer ensured that the king's wine and food were safe to eat and drink, and he enjoyed a position of trust. Due to his intimate contact with the king, the cupbearer often exerted significant political sway at court.

Nehemiah recognized that addressing the situation in Jerusalem could not be accomplished without sizable political support. He also understood his position in the royal court and used this to his utmost advantage. A sense of immediacy is in Nehemiah's actions; within only a few months of hearing the news about Jerusalem, Nehemiah developed and began to implement his strategic plan.

Nehemiah leveraged his position in court to ask for support from the one person who could make or break the project—the king. This was not a spur-of-the-moment request. He was well-prepared, developing a way for the king to think rebuilding the wall was his idea.

The king knew Nehemiah well enough to know that something was wrong. Showing great wisdom and restraint, Nehemiah waited for the king to question him. On the spot, he answered the king's specific questions on the timing and details of the proposed expedition. Nehemiah activated the support of the king, garnering money, materials, and safe passage to Jerusalem.

———

I once worked under a company president who was compared to the Pigpen character in the Snoopy comic strip series. Pigpen is a little boy who leaves a trail of dust wherever he goes. This man knew where we needed to go and how to get there. He was opinionated and decisive but highly well-respected.

Unfortunately, the speed at which he enacted decisions often left people scrambling to pick up the pieces after him, and this independent behavior ran afoul of the corporate offices. To his complete surprise, he was removed after only a few years. He had forgotten the importance of building and activating a support network within corporate headquarters.

The importance of having a support network became clear during my tenure as Chair of our leadership team at church. I believed I knew where we needed to be going and how to get there. I did not intend to act as a Lone Ranger, but I mistakenly approached our leadership team with fully hatched plans, expecting them to be wholeheartedly endorsed. It did not turn out well.

I quickly learned that building momentum and support for any idea took multiple side discussions. Listening and leaning into alternate thoughts and ideas was crucial. I discovered which voices on the leadership team carried the furthest and which provided the most insight.

Before approaching the leadership team as a whole, I met individually with those who had the most sway. Less resistance was achieved by establishing a broader base of support before bringing a plan forward for formal action, and the final project was typically much better than initially planned.

Take care to not work in a vacuum. Look around. You are in the best position to know the influencers within your differing circles of control. Recognize that each unique situation may require you to engage with a different support network. Be intentional about engaging with those who can affect the outcome you hope to achieve.

As you begin activating your networks, you will need to know what is negotiable and more importantly, what is not. Guide your conversations to areas where you are willing to accept input or help. Ask these people to speak into your specific situation, honoring what they bring. Remember that multiple conversations may be needed. Do not be in such a hurry to move forward on your own that you lose the help you need from others.

Leveraging support networks is all about seeking counsel. Invite the Holy Spirit to be present and speak through others. Remind yourself that you do not know it all. Psalm 32:8, "I will instruct you and teach you in the way which you should go; I will counsel you with My eye upon you." Listen carefully and allow God to guide you through the voices of others. A strong support network is critical to the success of any plan.

Trust but Verify

It is common for people who go through a particular situation to experience it quite differently from each other. Our reactions and responses are impacted by our personal perceptions and biases. What we believe we have seen or heard may be completely different from what others think they have seen or heard.

One well-known experiment, enacted in a schoolroom setting, teaches the danger of this. A student begins to grumble at those around them. The frustration escalates, the teacher notices, a full-out shouting match ensues, and the student storms out of the classroom, much to the astonishment of the other students. The teacher also storms out, leaving the remaining students to talk amongst themselves.

After a minute or two, the teacher returns and calmly asks each student to write what happened precisely. As the students share their experiences, it becomes evident that even within the same room, with everyone viewing the same situation, a significant disparity emerges between what each person perceived as truth.

Who has not experienced this in one form or another? You are given information that results in what you believe to be an obvious conclusion. However, new facts or information come to light that provide an alternate view. Had you known this information beforehand, your response might have been different. Wise leaders understand how critical it is to accurately assess a situation before acting.

Nehemiah had no reason to distrust his brother or compatriots; they had traveled 900 miles for help. They came with firsthand knowledge of the dangerous situation and conditions within Jerusalem. What they reported raised enough concern for Nehemiah to act.

Upon reaching Jerusalem, however, Nehemiah did not act immediately. He waited for three days after arriving before he and a handful of trusted men performed a complete (albeit stealthy) inspection of the walls and gates around Jerusalem in the middle of the night.

Welcome to the next leadership concept: trust but verify. Verification was vital to ensuring that Nehemiah had a correct understanding of the situation before doing anything else. He chose not to rely solely on one report.

In Nehemiah 2, we are introduced to two adversaries: Sanballat and Tobiah. Nehemiah 2:10 tells us that Nehemiah came to "seek the welfare of the sons of Israel." The same verse also informs us that this visit was "very displeasing" to these individuals who know that Nehemiah has come with the king's authorization. At this point, the wall is not even mentioned.

It is easy to imagine that Nehemiah was treated like royalty during those three days. Maybe they thought that they could flatter him with good food or finery. They most likely tried to alleviate any threat to their own positions of power while acknowledging he had been sent by the king.

What Nehemiah wanted, however, was to discern the truth about the condition of the wall and his people. Were his fellow citizens mistaken? What was the true extent of the damage?

As we seek to understand the extent of what we are facing, we need to train ourselves to come to each situation with the realization that we may not have all the facts or that sometimes our information may be based on rumor instead of truth. Independent assessment is prudent before action.

Keep in mind that deception may not be intentional. Someone may be so entangled in a situation that they cannot see beyond their own perception. Additional perspective or facts may be missing, which may be crucial for responding wisely. This is not to say that immediate action is never needed, but taking the time to pause, assess, and verify almost always leads to a more solid outcome.

I am the first to admit that I tend toward the immediate. I am a decisive individual and have been accused more than once of moving forward at a pace that leaves others behind. This can be frustrating for others and keep me from having all the information needed to chart a wise course of action.

When I became the Church Chair, I promised transparency and adherence to our Bylaws. This required us to refine and hone the framework of our organizational structure to bring it back into alignment with our Bylaws. Part of this reorganization included retiring several "rogue" ministries.

While there was nothing inherently wrong with these ministries, they were often so tied to one individual that if that person left or was no longer interested in leading that ministry, it would die. Evaluating each ministry with respect to our missional priorities allowed us to place each ministry squarely within a framework that ensured its long-term viability and support.

Enter my friend, "Joe." Joe is zealous about bringing others to Jesus. Joe also tends to do what he wants, with little regard for how he gets there. I was vexed when he announced to the congregation one Sunday that our church would engage in one of his projects. No one on our leadership team was aware of this project. No ministry team leaders were aware. No one, it seemed, but Joe.

Through this incident I learned the key concept of "trust but verify." The more I talked with others in our leadership, the more frustrated I became. It appeared that he was once again doing whatever he felt like doing. We had worked hard to reinstate our organizational structure, and he blatantly ignored it.

Not wanting our silence to be considered validation, I confronted him. I did not want his side of the story. I wanted him to get on board with our protocols, only to find that he had indeed checked with one of our pastors, who had given him permission for the project. That pastor, who was relatively new, had assumed that since we had endorsed this project previously, we would want to do it again. In deep shame, I apologized. I should have ensured I had all the facts before speaking.

Throughout the Bible, we are encouraged to be wise with the information we receive. "Every prudent man acts with knowledge but a fool displays folly" (Prov. 13:16). By taking time to verify what we think we know, we are on the pathway to acting honorably. The next time you hear something that requires action, take the extra step of verifying what you have heard. Only then should you plan your next step.

Rally the Troops

After leveraging your networks for support and verifying the situation, it is now time for the final step of your strategic plan: rallying those around you to action. The term "rally the troops" is used in war to boost soldiers' morale. It is a phrase that is intended to sustain a fighting spirit.

A common example is when a coach lights a fire under the team before a game starts or at halftime before they resume play. Have you ever wondered what words are spoken to create such a frenzied reaction?

Nehemiah's team are not soldiers who are accustomed to battle. Instead, he only has a defeated people who have returned to a destroyed homeland. The task appears overwhelming. Nehemiah does not have any troops to rebuild the wall; instead, he must rally those who are merely trying to stay alive.

Nehemiah's plan to rally his people includes acknowledging the truth of where they find themselves, offering a simple invitation to join, and casting a vision for the future. Then he turns from the actual situation to encourage them in their identity and calling.

Nehemiah does not sugar-coat the challenge. He clearly and directly tells the truth, "You see the bad situation we are in, that Jerusalem is desolate, and its gates burned by fire." (Neh. 2:17). The first point in rallying your troops is to acknowledge the situation exactly as it is.

Even though the people are already fully aware of what is around them, having a leader speak candidly about the reality of the situation builds trust. If a leader tells the truth now, people are ready to believe that the level of transparency will continue as the situation evolves.

In the *Harvard Business Review*, Judith Glaser writes,

As a leader, what you say and how you say it matters—especially when your company is facing challenge or crisis. Your job is to model what is right and good and energize the talent around you. If you don't, you will shut your employees down ("The Right Way to Rally your Troops" 09/13/2013).

This applies to any situation that you are leading.

Next, Nehemiah offers a simple invitation: "Come" (Neh. 2:17). His invitation is inclusive and simple. He invites them to participate by choosing to lead from their midst. Rebuilding the wall is not a bureaucratic order: he offers the people a place beside him. It is reminiscent of when Jesus says, "Come to me, all ..." (Matt. 11:28), an invitation that beckons to the core of our souls.

After speaking the truth and inviting the people to join, he shares his plan: "Let us rebuild the wall" (Neh. 2:17). He does not include details of how this will be accomplished. The people do not need that yet. Nor does he overcomplicate the plan; he simply appeals to what he knows is one of their deepest longings—safety and peace. The vision is cast.

He finishes by appealing to their identity and calling. Even in exile, they have not lost their identity as people of God. Even as they eke out a living in their broken homeland, that remains with them. The plea "that we may no longer be a reproach" (Neh. 2:17) resounds strongly. He testifies to the favor of their calling by both God and king.

Knowing that rebuilding the wall would create several powerful enemies, he recognizes that without the support of both the king and God, their chance of success was almost nonexistent. Invoking "for God and country" is the last piece needed to strengthen their resolve. They were not in this by themselves.

Truth-telling, invitation, vision, identity, and calling all work to create unity in purpose and a solidarity in approach that energizes and engages the people around Nehemiah's call to action. The troops have been rallied.

Several years ago, I was asked to fix a project at work. When I joined the team, the client had no intention of ever working with our firm again. We could not meet our schedule and were not providing our product. We were threatened with non-payment, anticipated a significant financial loss, and were being served with claims for delay. Employee morale was at an all-time low; people clamored to get reassigned to other projects.

Applying the concepts in this section, I began to rally the troops. I openly shared the extent of our struggles with the team, called on each person individually and invited them to engage in the common goal of catching up on our backlog and proactively completing our remaining work. We aligned our actions to only do what was needed to complete the project. We finished strong, making the client willing to work with us again.

Rolling up our sleeves and getting into the trenches with our people is needed. If we ever feel we are above others, we have already lost. As challenging situations arise, be the calm presence of truth. Most importantly, seek God's will. Allow Him to lead you and guide you in decisions you will need to make. Let Him show the timing of when to rally the troops.

The book of Joshua opens with just such a rally. God issues a charge to Joshua that is, in turn, passed to his men. "Have I not commanded you? Be strong and courageous! Do not tremble or be dismayed, for the Lord your God is with you wherever you go" (Josh. 1:9). This charge is what we can ultimately stand behind when we rally our people.

SUMMARY

This chapter taught us several vital components to developing a strategic protocol. First, activate your support networks. Do not try to develop a plan without the involvement of others.

Secondly, as difficult situations arise, be sure to fact-check. It is good—and necessary—to trust your friends and advisors, but do not be afraid to go on a personal fact-finding mission to ensure you understand the breadth of the situation before you act.

Finally, a strategic plan includes rallying those around you by being a ninja in truth-telling and inviting others to work alongside you. Equally valuable is being simple and direct in laying out the goal, appealing to what will strike a chord with your supporters, and above all, ensuring you align with where God is leading.

As situations unfold, be willing to invest in the concepts in this chapter to further develop your ability to lead at the precise place God has you. All the strategic planning in the world will not help you if you are unwilling to follow through and engage directly in the situation. Be bold when it is time to step out in faith and act.

CONSIDER

Reflecting on a current or recent crisis in your life, consider the role that listening plays in each of the three situational leadership concepts in this chapter: activate support, trust but verify, and rally the troops. How do listening and strategic planning work together?

PRAYER

Dear Jesus, when a crisis comes, may I not procrastinate. Help me to be wise enough to know when to seek the input of others or to gather more information before charging ahead. I pray that You will allow me to be known for being honest and willing to be in the trenches with everyone else. Give me the vision for where You are leading, particularly in the hard places. Most of all, I pray my response to any situation reflects Your calling on my life. Amen.

~3~

Structured Responsibilities

And next to him the men of Jericho built, and next to them
Zaccur the sons of Imri built (Neh. 3:2).

WITH APPROXIMATELY 2.3 MILLION YOUTH and one million
adult participants, the Boy Scouts of America (BSA) is argu-
ably one of the largest youth organizations in America today.
Yet, only 4 percent of those who enter the program earn the
prestigious rank of Eagle Scout.

Eagle Scouts are disproportionately represented in leadership positions in the military, academia, white-collar careers,
the clergy, business, and politics, as indicated in "Scouting's
Bottom Line" (U.S. Scouting Service Project, 2007), which
notes that Eagle Scouts account for:

64% of Air Force Academy graduates
68% of West Point graduates
70% of Annapolis graduates
72% of Rhodes Scholars
85% of FBI agents
26 of the first 29 astronauts

The lifetime rank of Eagle Scouts includes presidents, gov-
ernors, politicians, and CEOs of major corporations (e.g., Wal-
Mart, Marriott International). Why do Eagle Scouts rise to

such distinction? Without a doubt, leadership is a crucial component. Throughout every level of BSA, leadership opportunities and training abound, being infused into each rank and position in the organization.

The last step in becoming an Eagle Scout is to perform a culminating Service Project. This Service Project is considered proof of a Scout's ability to develop, plan, organize, and execute a project that benefits the community.

Rebuilding the wall around Jerusalem was an enormous Service Project that included all components necessary for any modern-day Boy Scout to earn the Eagle Scout rank. The primary focus of Nehemiah 3 is a documentation of how this public works project was organized.

Understanding the enormity of the task is essential. The wall is believed to have been 2.5 miles long, approximately eight feet thick, and an average height of forty feet. Originally boasting thirty-four watchtowers and nine gates, Nehemiah's task focused on rebuilding the entire perimeter of the wall, six gates, and the governor's residence.

In addition to constructing entirely new portions of the wall, many sections were in disrepair and needed to be rebuilt or strengthened. The stability of the remaining wall would have been questionable, and those approaching the work would have been required to have the skills to determine the extent of demolition before the wall could be rebuilt.

The most impressive part of this project was that it was completed in only fifty-two days—a success by any measure of definition.

This chapter presents three principal situational leadership concepts, focused on a life of boundaries, that improve the chances of success: clear delineation of individual responsibility, utilization of willing people regardless of background or skillset, and the importance of giving others the benefit of the doubt.

Divide and Conquer

The phrase "divide and conquer" usually refers to an offensive strategy that keeps an enemy from being able to unite against its attackers. The original motto, "divide and rule," is attributed to Philip II of Macedon around 350 BC. This earlier strategy separated groups of people to prevent alliances, as independent entities were easier to control or rule.

The earliest documentation of the application of "divide and conquer" as a military strategy is found in a book entitled *The Art of War* (1521) by Machiavelli. However, multiple examples show it was employed much earlier, even if not identified as such.

A divided military line having to protect numerous fronts simultaneously was easier to overcome. This concept is still utilized by military strategists today. Over the years, it has even expanded in application to foreign policy and politics.

Nehemiah's brilliance showed in his employing this tactic in the rebuilding effort. His reconnaissance had given him a solid understanding of the extent of the required repairs. Rather than sequentially rebuilding the wall, with each segment completed before work on the next section began, Nehemiah divided the project into approximately forty separate sections, with each sector starting simultaneously.

The intent was to complete as much as possible, as quickly as possible. An unfinished wall was no better than no wall. Until it was complete, it would offer no protection for the people. Rebuilding multiple sections simultaneously gave substantial momentum and energy to the project.

To recognize the scale of this project, consider the following: repairing 2.5 miles of wall in fifty-two days required that each section be rebuilt at a rate of just over six feet per day, seven days a week. That equated to moving and placing 75 cubic yards of rock and rubble, nearly 180 tons of material, each day.

Years ago, we ordered ten cubic yards of bark mulch for our yard. It took us weeks to move that pile, wheelbarrow by wheelbarrow. Granted, only two of us did the work, but I cannot imagine a pile of rock over seven times that size delivered and moved completely, seven days a week, nonstop, for almost two months. Both the undertaking and required workforce are beyond my imagination.

Nehemiah relied upon the established organization within Jerusalem, using separate people groups to deliver and complete each segment. There was no fighting over control or leadership. The divide-and-conquer approach allowed simple execution of each assignment.

Each group knew its specific area of responsibility. One team under Baruch's leadership was even praised for "zealously" repairing their section (Neh. 3:20). These people were motivated!

———

Teamwork is still touted today. From school assignments to job interviews, a team approach is expected. Interviewers often ask pointed questions to understand how someone may blend into an existing team. A recognition of the different stages of team building allows leaders to understand the health of their teams at any point of a project and adjust accordingly.

Work proposals often ask for examples of previous experience working with other team members. Submissions that do not lay out a robust teamwork approach rarely succeed. But even more critical than a team approach is the division of responsibility within that team. Teams are most efficient when responsibilities are clearly delineated and people are empowered to live within those boundaries.

Several years ago, I was the proposed project manager for a new bridge in downtown Seattle. Our team was well-prepared as we headed into the interview—until they threw us a curve ball. We were given ten minutes to develop a risk assessment for a tunnel rather than a bridge at the proposed location. Through this portion of the interview, the client walked around our team, listening to our conversations as we approached this challenge.

I believe the key to winning the project was employing a divide-and-conquer technique. We did not try to tackle the whole tunnel concept as one group. Instead, I divided our team into separate work groups to discuss different aspects of a tunnel alternative, assigned time for each group, and let them work independently.

We came back together, put the pieces in place, and provided a recommendation. The city was not looking for the best technical answer; they wanted to understand how we would work together as a team to approach the unique challenges they knew the project would encounter.

The same principle applies to working through any project or task you may encounter. Many hands make light work. However, chaos can ensue unless those many hands are managed with a clear delineation of each person's responsibilities and limits. Organizing for success often requires parsing out tasks. Keeping the focus on the end goal allows everyone else to focus on their specific tasks.

Jesus has given different talents to His people expecting

each person to live up to the gift and responsibility they have been given. These giftings can be considered a delineation of our responsibility. "Now these are the gifts Christ gave to the church: the apostles, the prophets, the evangelists, and the pastors and teachers" (Eph. 4:11). We are encouraged to harness the gifts of those around us.

The next verse states the end goal, "Their responsibility is to equip God's people to do His work and build up the church, the body of Christ" (Eph. 4:12). We should never take our eyes off the goal, regardless of the path to get there, working within the limits and boundaries He has provided.

All-Hands-On-Deck

The *Merriam-Webster* dictionary defines all-hands-on-deck as "of, relating to, or being a situation in which every available person is needed or called to assist." Historically, this term was first used to call for all members of a ship's crew to come to the deck, usually in a time of crisis.

I have many memories of my father, who served in the Naval Air Force during the Korean War, using a cousin of this term, "muster on the quarter-deck," to indicate the need for our entire family to come immediately. It was the same concept: everyone was needed right away.

I had always associated these terms with the word crisis until I looked at available articles and books centered around an all-hands-on-deck approach to leadership. I noticed two distinct lines of thought: crisis management and teamwork.

In crisis management, all associated individuals—even those involved remotely—are expected to pitch in until the crisis is resolved. An example of this is when there is a deadline at work. Those engaged in the project must work late nights and long hours to meet the schedule.

This approach tends to be temporary in nature; people resume their regular routine when the crisis passes. Deadlines can require an enormous outlay of energy that is typically unsustainable in the long run. The pressure that is created on individuals to produce is extremely taxing. Multiple back-to-back situations with an all-hands-on-deck approach can lead to burnout.

The other idea behind this saying is along the lines of cooperative teamwork. "All hands on deck" is simply a call for everyone to participate. A feeling of camaraderie is developed. Everyone feels that they are needed to accomplish a successful outcome.

"All-hands" meetings are now a recognized and often routine part of our work lives. These meetings are simply a chance for everyone to be together and hear messages from management at once. No crisis must be present, but the sense of working together to achieve success remains a critical component.

Nehemiah approached rebuilding the wall from a crisis management perspective. In the next chapter, we will find significant opposition to rebuilding the wall. All gates needed to be installed and functioning as soon as possible. Without an all-hands-on-deck approach, the wall and gates would never have been completed in fifty-two days.

Nehemiah always kept his focus on the end goal. How he got there or who worked on the wall was not as crucial as completing it. The list of people involved in this project is extensive: high priests, priests, Levites, men of Israel, daughters, district officials, goldsmiths, perfumers, temple servants, and merchants.

While some of these people may have had experience in manual labor, the majority would not necessarily have had wall repair on their resumé. The variety of those who assisted provides a unique perspective on the meaning of servanthood. When Nehemiah called, they responded.

Recall from Chapter 1 that the very first concept we explored was the critical nature of our identity. From priests to merchants, the essence of those who returned from exile was deeply ingrained. When the call came, they were ready. Whether they had skills for building a wall did not matter. They were willing to aid with everything they had.

Not long ago, our church went through a major crisis as our newly installed Lead Pastor was diagnosed with and battled pancreatic cancer. During his twenty-one-month journey, our congregation learned what it meant to respond and support him as needs arose. Although he had already moved to Seattle from Sacramento when he received the diagnosis, his house had not been sold, and his family had not yet joined him.

He chose to not accept the offer to return to Sacramento but let us go through this trial with him. It was a time of incredible growth for our congregation. We learned that we all had something to contribute.

We held multiple corporate fasts, embraced intercessory prayer, rotated driving him to chemo, laid hands on him, covered when he was too weak to preach, brought meals, fixed things around his home, and prayed and prayed. All the while, he became more and more embedded into the fabric of his new church.

Though fatiguing, it was all hands on deck, day after day, month after month. It was a privilege. None of us knew what we were doing, but he and his family accepted what we had to offer and let us fully participate.

As tasks or projects arise, keeping an all-hands-on-deck attitude will help welcome everyone who desires to participate and help. We are not called to be selective. Even if someone is not our first choice, we are to engage their earnest desire to serve, remembering that they are not serving us—they are serving Jesus. Sometimes a specific skill set is needed, but overall, when we have a task to accomplish and we are making a call for all hands on deck, be careful to not judge or refuse to let others join.

Revelation 7:9 states, "After this I saw a vast crowd, too great to count, from every nation and tribe and people and language, standing in front of the throne and before the Lamb." Jesus is not selective but accepts all people who desire to serve Him with whatever gifts they have been given. If Jesus is willing to welcome everyone in His kingdom so freely, can we do less?

The Benefit of the Doubt

As Nehemiah continued organizing and planning, a situation arose with the wall section assigned to the Tekoite people, who lived just over eleven miles from Jerusalem. We are told that "their nobles did not support the work of their masters" (Neh. 3:5). This is the only recorded example of discord between those working on the wall and their leaders.

We are not given the reason for their opposition. Work may have been needed in their village, or there may have been an economic impact with the people working elsewhere for an unknown period. Or the nobles may even have been allied with Nehemiah's enemies. Regardless of the reason, the discord was noteworthy enough to be recorded.

With the rebuilding only beginning to get underway, it would have been easy for Nehemiah to send the workers home and reassign that wall section to another group without impacting his schedule. That decision would have kept him on good terms with the upper class citizens in Tekoa.

Allowing the Tekoites to continue working on the wall impacted diplomatic relations with the nobles. However, Nehemiah did not send them home but allowed them to continue.

Situations often pop up to disturb our well-laid plans. Taking the easy route can be attractive. Given Nehemiah's plight, many of us might have given in to the complaints of the nobles, justifying this course of action in the name of keeping the peace. The wall would still have been completed with the bonus of harmony with the nobles of Tekoa.

Nehemiah chose the more difficult path. He was not swayed by outside forces nor by the nobles' displeasure. Remember, he was there on the king's business! If the nobles did not want to support the wall repairs, they would answer to King Artaxerxes, not Nehemiah.

Nehemiah was not a risk-taker. His entire approach to getting King Artaxerxes' support and enlisting the people of Jerusalem in the rebuilding effort was carefully designed for maximum effect. Why would he risk potential discord with these nobles or a disruption in the schedule, by allowing this one group to continue? Nehemiah modeled how to give others the benefit of the doubt.

Nehemiah had performed an independent assessment of the wall after arriving in Jerusalem, and he also assessed the situation with the Tekoites to gain firsthand knowledge of their true motivation for participating in this project.

Nehemiah did not judge or hold them accountable for the lack of support from their nobles. Rather, after this assessment, not only did the Tekoites continue with their assigned section of the wall, but they were also the only named group that was given a second section of the wall to repair (Neh. 3:27).

Giving others the benefit of the doubt can be challenging, particularly when someone is not doing something they said they would. At times, it might seem easier to step in and do it ourselves if others are not performing. We will most likely end up with exactly what we want when we want it.

The downside of this approach and the damage it can cause cannot be overemphasized. Others may no longer feel needed or be reluctant to volunteer if they know you will take over. The burden can become excessive; resentment can build. Additionally, an "I will do it myself" pace cannot be kept up forever. Burnout results.

Rather than stepping in when someone is underperforming or trying to block our plans, our responsibility is to determine the underlying reason. Assume positive intent and work to understand what is happening behind the scenes. Has there been poor guidance? Are they lacking needed tools or resources? Are there external pressures you could help alleviate? Giving others the benefit of the doubt allows the work to be distributed fairly and empowers people to feel valued as team members.

If you are unwilling to give others the benefit of the doubt, you could be keeping someone from growing in new ways or keeping them from God's blessing. We must guard against becoming a stumbling block. God may want to speak or teach through a situation, or He may be planning to use that task to encourage others to become more motivated to serve Him.

I am currently taking a God-directed one-year sabbatical

from church leadership. As this year has progressed, I have seen others step into gaps that arose when I left. Seeing others begin to use their gifts in ways that were not possible when I was doing a lot of the work brings joy as I see them being blessed for their participation. I gave others the benefit of the doubt, and they stepped up.

Jesus always looked beyond the exterior of each person He encountered, focusing on their motivation. Consider the example in Luke 10 of Zacchaeus, the corrupt tax collector who collected more than he was due. Zacchaeus had gone so far as to climb a tree to be able to see Jesus through the crowds. Jesus wasn't concerned about what society thought of Zacchaeus. Instead, He called to him to come down, setting in motion a life-changing encounter.

This Scripture ends with Jesus reminding us that "the Son of Man came to seek and to save the lost" (Luke 19:10). Taking the time to see beyond the surface and giving the benefit of the doubt to better understand the rationale or motivation of those who want to serve can open an opportunity for others to encounter Jesus in a new way.

SUMMARY

Organizational clarity is required for any endeavor. Having a clear division of responsibility and boundaries allows work to proceed smoothly. Understanding the organizational framework within which we engage is essential for any task, large or small.

This is particularly true in times of crisis where situational leadership may be required. We explored several leadership concepts that can easily be applied by anyone looking to come out on the other side of a crisis intact. Using these concepts will further develop your ability to lead through each situation.

The concept of "divide and conquer" can be used to break down overwhelming tasks into smaller, manageable pieces for any situation and helps everyone involved know what their exact responsibilities are. We must be willing to recognize that sometimes we need help. In these cases, utilize your support network, allowing others to step in and help regardless of their background or skillset. Do not try to do everything by yourself. Learning to give others the benefit of the doubt may be an opportunity for blessing.

Consider

Regardless of our place in life, each of us has one or more areas of structured responsibility. How do the situational leadership concepts of divide and conquer, all hands on deck, and giving others the benefit of the doubt shape your responsibilities? Can you apply the boundaries provided by these concepts to a pressing situation in your life?

Prayer

Heavenly Father, give me the wisdom to know when and how to build a structured response to crisis that involves the giftedness of others. Keep my focus on helping others learn how to engage and understand their boundaries. May I not step in and take over but rather encourage and lead others in a way that allows them to achieve their best for You. Give me the boldness needed to see others as You see them, helping them pursue new opportunities. Amen.

4

External Assaults

And all of them conspired together to come and fight against Jerusalem and to cause a disturbance in it. But we prayed to our God, and because of them we set up a guard against them day and night (Neh. 4:8–9).

You do not have to look far to find examples of those who have overcome incredible odds to achieve greatness. Be it the story of a stranger, friend, or family member, we are never far from encountering someone who has persevered through overwhelming difficulties. How we respond to attack or trial is a critical component of leadership. Will we give up or stay the course?

Adrianne Haslet-Davis lost her leg in the deadly 2013 Boston Marathon bombing. In 2016, she ran the 26.2-mile course with a prosthetic limb to raise money for Limbs for Life. Her endurance through tremendous odds is truly inspirational. She learned firsthand that responding to external attacks meant perseverance, not retreat.

Three of Nehemiah's opponents were briefly introduced at the end of Nehemiah 2: Sanballat the Horonite, Tobiah the Ammonite, and Geshem the Arab. The Horonites and Ammonites were two groups that had been driven out of the Promised

Land by the Israelites. Arabs are descended from Ishmael, Abraham's first son, who was exiled into the desert in favor of Isaac, the father of Israel. No love was lost between any of these people.

At the end of Nehemiah 2, these three men "mocked and despised" Nehemiah and his men. They claimed that rebuilding the wall would be an act of rebellion against King Artaxerxes (Neh. 2:19). Nehemiah's terse response was to proclaim God's favor for the Israelites. He reminded the men that the cultural and spiritual divide between them and the Israelites was deep and abiding. They would have "no portion, right, or memorial in Jerusalem" (Neh. 2:20).

The intrigues between these three men and Nehemiah pick back up in Nehemiah 4, where we get our first glimpse into the reality of what it meant for the Israelites to overcome incredible odds to rebuild the wall while living among enemies.

Why these men fought against Nehemiah so vehemently is obvious. Rebuilding the wall would have threatened those in power, and power is a strong motivator. Regardless of their initial reception of Nehemiah, a threat to their power turned them into adversaries.

Power still motivates people today. We recognize that Satan does not care about stagnant people. Those who are not growing in their faith pose no concern. Those willing to stand firm amid opposition to the gospel are perceived as a threat.

Being God's people and following where He leads does not mean everything will be miraculously easy. If we choose to stand for Jesus, mocking will come. As Christians, we are called to persevere. This chapter explores the relational leadership principles focusing on a life of protection, particularly for those within our circles of influence.

The first concept teaches us to recognize when mocking

has become dangerous and action is required. We then implement a rally point to protect those in our care. The final concept is how to stay the course Jesus has set, not letting down our guard, particularly as we encounter difficulties.

Sticks and Stones

The saying "Sticks and stones may break my bones, but names will never hurt me" is an old chant taught to children to defend themselves against name-calling or verbal bullying. The statement is meant to imply that verbal abuse or taunts cannot hurt the child in the same way that physical harm may.

Anyone who has been a recipient of verbal abuse knows this is not true, regardless of how many times one repeats or tries to convince themselves that these words are valid. Words do indeed hurt and often remain with a child throughout their life. They can demoralize a child, making them even more susceptible to the potential for further abuse.

Nehemiah 4 opens with Sanballat and Tobiah mocking and hurling abuse at the Israelites. Their anger has spurred them to ridicule the work being done. Although Nehemiah leaned into his go-to response of immediately turning to God for help, he also recognized the toll the mocking was taking on the people, telling God that the mocking has "demoralized the builders" (Neh. 4:5).

Despite the verbal bullying, the people worked "with all their heart" and built the wall to half its height. Only as the breaches in the wall began to close did the attacks move from verbal abuse to tangible threats of physical violence. The mocking had turned the corner and become dangerous. It could no longer be ignored.

Verbal abuse has a significant and long-lasting impact on our psyches. Prolonged or extended periods of abuse impact our responses. In Nehemiah 4, the demoralizing spirit that was being relentlessly sown by the mocking resulted in a reaction of overwhelming fear.

The workers were so fearful that they issued a report throughout Judah saying, "We ourselves are unable to rebuild the wall" (Neh. 4:10). The long hours, the enormity of the task, and the mocking took their toll. When the threat of physical attack was added, it was too much to endure. The workers came to Nehemiah ten separate times to report death threats. The warning was acute—attacks were coming. They were ready to give up.

We learn two things from this passage. First, we must expect external assaults, even when things seems to be operating smoothly. We should never be surprised when we encounter resistance or an outright attack. First Peter 5:8 reminds us that we are to "Be of sober spirit, be on the alert. Your adversary, the devil, prowls about like a roaring lion, seeking someone to devour."

We would be foolish to ignore this warning. Attacks come in many forms. Recognize that Satan seeks to destroy any person or institution actively serving and living for Jesus. Be wary. Be watchful. Be expectant. As these attacks come, be ready with a game plan to counter them.

Secondly, we must recognize when a threat has moved to the realm where physical danger is possible. Something that may have started out as minor resistance may eventually feed into something that puts us, our families, our leaders, or even our churches in physical harm.

Many Christians are unwilling to recognize that we live in a post-Christian era in the US, wistfully remembering a bygone era where most people went to church on Sundays or freely identified as Christians. People identifying themselves as either unchurched or nonreligious are becoming increasingly common.

In the United States, few Christians expect to encounter external, physical assaults against themselves or their churches. Yet year after year, the threat has grown to the point where it is no longer an anomaly to read about a church shooting or buildings being vandalized or burned. We must be awake and ready for this possibility.

Many of us may have wondered what our response would be if our lives were on the line for Jesus. Jesus says, "For whoever wishes to save his life shall lose it; but whoever loses his life for My sake and the gospel's shall save it" (Mark 8:35). While we pray that we will never be tested in this way, are you willing to be faithful through each circumstance regardless of the result?

Currently, the church in the U.S. is not a primary target for external attacks. Most people who disagree with Christian beliefs just stay away. The likelihood is low that I will ever be confronted with a physical altercation due to my religious beliefs. However, there is a growing recognition that even if a church has not experienced an external clash, the church at large is under attack.

External assaults are not the only concern. More and more are coming directly from inside the church. Dividing issues are pulling at the very fabric of the church. What was once held tightly as biblically grounded beliefs are being questioned. Slow desensitization to what the Bible calls sin is happening, with biblical truth reinterpreted in the name of love and inclusive acceptance of all beliefs or norms.

First Peter 5:9 guides us in how we should respond to any form of assault: "But resist him, firm in your faith, knowing that the same experiences of suffering are being accomplished by your brethren who are in the world." We are not alone and not the only ones under attack. We must stand firm in our faith and solidarity with our brothers and sisters elsewhere. Someday, it may be our turn.

When you encounter opposition, do not try to handle it by yourself. Be willing to reach out to others who have had the same experiences and let them walk alongside you, providing insight and guidance, particularly in the aftermath of an assault when you begin picking up the pieces again. Hold on to the knowledge that you are not alone.

Rally Point

When my children were young, a white dogwood tree stood in the front yard. That dogwood tree had many purposes. We lived on a main street with many cars passing by each day. The kids knew that when they rode their tricycles in the driveway or played in the front yard, they were not allowed to go beyond the line of the dogwood tree.

An invisible fence was cast along the front of our property to protect the children from errant cars or people. It also served as our rally point in case of fire—or any situation that might necessitate us getting out of the house quickly. We all knew that the tree was our meeting point. For me, that tree symbolized safety. Seeing it in the front yard each day gave me a feeling of security.

In Nehemiah 4, the threats against the Israelites had reached a point where further progress on the wall was jeopardized unless something was done. Nehemiah took immediate action by posting guards in the lowest parts and exposed places of the wall. By securing the areas most vulnerable to attack, the people were willing to return to work.

Even with these defenses in place, Nehemiah recognized that it was virtually impossible to simultaneously defend the entire wall length. It would have been a tremendous waste of human resources as it was unlikely that multiple assaults would coincide.

With work areas spread out along the length of the wall, the people were separated. So, Nehemiah implemented the concept of a rallying point. He stationed a trumpeter to be on alert, and when an attack began, the trumpet would sound. All men would "rally to us there" (Neh. 4:20). Rather than spreading their defenses too thinly, this allowed the work to continue with the knowledge that everyone would help everyone else whenever and wherever the next assault occurred.

Nehemiah also recognized that attacks could occur at night when the Israelites were sleeping and relatively defenseless. He called for the people to spend the night in Jerusalem with the servants standing guard so that the laborers were refreshed for the next day. Pulling them all to one rally point inside the partially rebuilt walls offered a measure of protection that could not be obtained by being randomly scattered across the countryside in the evenings.

Most buildings have a physical rally point or action plan in the event of a fire, tornado, or other danger. Similarly, we need to develop rallying points against spiritual assault to ensure the safety of those we lead. Like Nehemiah, we are to shore up our defenses and provide protection to those serving with us. When anyone we know is under attack, we must rally around that person.

When our lead pastor became gravely ill, we hired an interim associate pastor to assist with some pastoral responsibilities, including weekly preaching. She was charged with maintaining and advancing our missional priorities, hoping that he would return to the pulpit someday. After he passed, she stepped into a de facto interim lead pastor role while searching for our next lead pastor.

About two months after she took on that expanded role, she and her family began to undergo spiritual attacks that took the form of physical ordeals. She and her husband have four children, and except for one child, they all suffered various physical issues, necessitating multiple ambulance rides and over a dozen emergency room visits. It was beyond coincidental. She and her family were under spiritual assault due to her position in our church.

After one particularly brutal episode, our church went into action. Those gifted in intercessory prayer gathered by phone and outside her home. As she walked through each room of her house, we spent time praying for protection over each occupant and space in the home, including the attic and yard. We stepped into the gap and shored up the walls of protection around her. She and her family became the rallying point for our prayers.

With COVID-19 still raging in our country, we need to recognize that not meeting together for worship is as dangerous as meeting together physically. It is easy to stray when we are alone and without support. The technology that allows online meetings and worship has become critical to staying connected. It is too easy to become complacent when we are disconnected.

To counter complacency, we need to be aware that it is happening. We must learn to become attuned to the spiritual life of those around us. Notice and be mindful of the spiritual condition of others. Ask people about their walk with Jesus, and then listen carefully.

As you sense spiritual battles, help to lead them back toward Jesus. He is the ultimate rallying point. Jesus says, "I am the way the truth and the life. No one comes to the Father but through me" (John 14:6). As we continue to turn toward and focus our lives on following Him, we recognize that our ultimate safety and protection are in His hands. We are to simply acknowledge and turn to Him as our rallying point in every situation.

En Guarde!

Alexander Dumas' book, *The Three Musketeers*, is a thrilling tale of blackmail, betrayal, greed, chivalry, and love. The sword fights were always my favorite parts of the action-adventure film based on the book. The physical exertion and stamina required are incredible. As a child, I remember carrying a stick around and pretending to be a musketeer. I would call out "on guard" to unsuspecting trees and bushes, mercilessly stabbing them in the name of justice.

While it is fun to watch swordplay in a movie, the reality is that a sword was a practical weapon of protection in the days of Nehemiah. The Israelites' danger had not subsided, and guards were placed at a weak end along the wall. In addition to the workers rallying wherever needed at the sound of the trumpet, Nehemiah required that "those who were rebuilding the wall and those who carried burdens took their load with one hand doing the work and the other holding a weapon" (Neh. 4:17).

Nehemiah 4:23 states that weapons were carried "even to the water." Half of the servants worked while half held spears, shields, bows, and breastplates. The workers were instructed to always keep their weapons ready. How could this not have impacted their work? Yet, it did not. As noted earlier, this major feat of labor was accomplished—even with the challenge of being always armed—in only fifty-two days.

During this time of potential danger and attack, Nehemiah did not offensively try to remove the threat. When a threat emerges, we often try to figure out ways to countermand the impending assault. We can become so fixated on the threat and its potential impact on our objective that we lose our focus on the mission itself.

Nehemiah did the opposite. Although he was ready to provide defense when needed, he did not lose focus. Rebuilding the wall was his one and only goal. Everything else, threats included, was secondary. Not only did Nehemiah maintain focus, but he also did not sway from the original plan or organizational structure he had implemented. He did not let down his guard while staying the course.

It is popular for churches to revisit their values or mission statements regularly. The idea is to keep the wording and ideas fresh, new, and culturally relevant. Typically, this will happen on an approximate three-year cycle. Leaders are looking for a hook to attract outsiders and keep people coming back. They become so eager to engage others with a catchy slogan (with just the right words!) that they lose concentration on their mission.

In the book of Hebrews, we are encouraged to maintain our focus solely on Jesus.

> *Therefore, since we are surrounded by such a huge crowd of witnesses to the life of faith, let us strip off every weight that slows us down, especially the sin that so easily trips us up. And let us run with endurance the race God has set before us. We do this by keeping our eyes on Jesus, the champion who initiates and perfects our faith* (Heb 12:1–2 NLT).

We are each to understand our mission in life and then maintain an undivided focus on that mission. God has called and placed you exactly where you need to be at this time in your life to allow Him to work through you. You may not be in a formal leadership position; however, the call for you to follow Him considers all your unique pieces of self that allow you to serve Him in a way that only you can.

Take a deep look to ensure you have not shifted from what you believe God has called you to do, i.e., your missional priorities. This does not mean that things should never change. It means that change should be based solely on where Jesus is leading, not what others may be telling you to do. Let us look at a practical example.

Several years ago, our youth pastor decided to phase out our Vacation Bible School (VBS) programming—a decision that was controversial. While considered successful based on the number of children who attended, we knew that many parents used the program for a week of free childcare during the summer. Additionally, statistics showed very few families joined our church because of this program.

With a deep dive into child development research, our youth pastor helped our leadership team reimagine a children's ministry that was multi-generational. It allowed evening classes so parents could participate, one that tied more clearly to our existing tutoring program for elementary children, who were already within our walls.

Knowing that discontinuing VBS would allow us to remain more in line with our focus on our missional priority of following Jesus helped us when the attacks came. We knew what we were doing and why. It was an intentional choice that was supported by our entire leadership team.

It was not about one person trying to change what we were doing. Our entire leadership team was armed with the knowledge needed to remain focused and unified as pressure mounted and then subsided. We stayed the course.

Staying the course sometimes means we must change what or how we have always done things. It is not about stubbornly holding onto the past but about being willing to identify what might be pulling us away or distracting us from where God is leading.

Countering potential mission drift is an essential leadership skill that we need to master in our lives. Doing so and letting others see the process you are undergoing allows this process to become a training ground for them too.

Summary

We must guard against complacency in our faith. Those who actively pursue God's mission will encounter external attacks. The relational leadership concepts in this chapter explore how you can develop protection against these assaults, both for yourself and others.

People who follow Jesus are not immune from danger. We should not be surprised by either physical or spiritual threats.

Standing firm requires more than just discipline and a single-minded focus; we should use the opportunity to band with others.

As danger presents itself, the concept of keeping Jesus as our rally point becomes critical. We must not allow ourselves to be pulled away from our calling. We are to counter any potential mission drift by identifying and defusing distractions.

Think about the relationships in your life and how the concepts within this chapter can be applied to help you lead through external assaults that come through these relationships. Mastering these approaches will allow you to protect those around you, whether in your family, on a leadership team, or even in the worldwide church.

CONSIDER

As we consider our changing world, the idea of external attacks against Christians is no longer baseless. What relational leadership concepts will protect you against future physical and spiritual assaults? Identify specific ways to lead with the proper protection, a rally strategy, and a firm focus on Jesus.

PRAYER

Lord God, help me maintain my focus, so I am not distracted from what You have called me to do. Open my eyes to recognize spiritual attacks and bind Your people together in unity, so we stay the course even in difficult times. I want to stand for You even when it becomes dangerous. Help me to not let down my guard but to take Your warnings seriously and to not be more focused on doing ministry than on serving You. Amen.

≈5≈

Inner Turmoil

Remember me, O my God, for good, according to all that I have done for this people (Neh. 5:19).

WHY DO YOU DO WHAT YOU DO? What has drawn you to that role? These questions go beyond any background or training you may have and even go beyond personality styles. These questions get to the heart of the biggest "why" you can ask yourself for any endeavor you undertake—what motivates you? Spend a bit of time thinking about this question.

Naming dozens of great leaders throughout history is easy: Martin Luther, Mahatma Gandhi, Winston Churchill, and Mother Teresa. The list is seemingly endless and crosses the spectrums of race, position, and wealth. Great leaders are often also assumed to be good. However, a list can just as easily be made of people who did not work for the good of humanity: Joseph Stalin, Adolph Hitler, and Genghis Khan.

A quick Google search provides information on the achievements of each of these named leaders. We can learn all about their lives and actions. However, discerning their inner motivation is more complicated. Why did they do what they did? What drove them?

My sister often tells me that I am driven. Sitting still is

difficult for me. Something always needs to be done. One of my husband's hobbies is watching a movie every night. While I do not enjoy television, I choose to enter his world by watching something with him a few nights each week. But even then, it is not unusual for me to knit, sew, or straighten the house during this time, often resulting in my hearing, "Would you please just sit down!" What motivates me toward continuous activity? What drives me?

Most people with any biblical familiarity would include Nehemiah in a list of leaders, including Moses, King David, or Simon Peter. He has all the marks of a fantastic leader: decisiveness, action, drive, organizational excellence, the strength of purpose, and military strategy.

Nehemiah 5 gives us a rare glimpse into the motivation behind his leadership. Simply put, everything he does is for the people, not himself. Nehemiah is not looking for glory or personal gain. He leads because God has called him to rebuild the wall. He puts everything in himself concerning leadership at God's disposal; he simply and humbly allows God to use him for the benefit of the people.

Chapter 4 ended with a well-developed strategy to handle external threats. Now, as we turn to Nehemiah 5, we receive insight into Nehemiah's motivation and the state of the people. If we expected smooth sailing internally, we would be wrong.

In this chapter, Nehemiah teaches us relational leadership concepts that address turmoil within our walls, handling those who are only out for themselves, and ways to help others pull their own weight.

Turmoil Within

Several years ago, I moved to a new company after almost twenty-eight years of employment at one firm. Although I liked my job at the first firm, I had moved up within the organization to the point of daily interaction with corporate leadership. I began to question the values I was encountering. Eventually, I looked elsewhere and moved to a new firm.

The new company held all the promises of Eden. A new position with good pay, this job had challenging responsibilities, opportunities for growth, and regular interaction with senior leadership. However, as the company had grown, it had not adjusted to what was required to manage or lead increasingly more prominent projects.

It seemed a perfect fit for my background as I began implementing new project management and quality processes. Unfortunately, although everyone was friendly, no one really wanted me there. They were so comfortable doing things the old way that the last thing they wanted was someone stirring the pot.

So, I began to listen. Intentionally traveling to all the offices in North America and meeting with the leaders allowed me to better understand the unique challenges each was facing. It allowed me to implement the needed changes in a way that connected with their differing needs. While some pushback remained, the relationships I built on those trips helped build trust in what I was doing.

In 2017, a survey of pastors identified Andy Stanley as one of the ten most influential living pastors in America. One of his oft-quoted sayings is, "Leaders who don't listen will eventually be surrounded by people who have nothing to say."

Nehemiah 5 begins with an accounting of a tremendous burden that had been placed on the people. Only once the external risks were effectively countered did this inner turmoil come to light. The people cried out against their Jewish brothers with four explicit charges: not enough food to eat, mortgaging homes and lands for food, borrowing money to pay taxes, and selling children into indentured service to make ends meet.

Rather than everyone sharing and pulling together in the effort to rebuild the wall, we see distinct "haves" and "have nots." Some Jews were becoming well-off at the expense of other Jews. So, in addition to the people struggling to maintain physical safety from external threats, internal discord flourished. They were barely surviving with no end in sight.

Nehemiah addressed this first and foremost by listening and defusing this potentially explosive situation. Nehemiah stated that he "was very angry when I had heard their outcry and these words" (Neh. 5:6). Nehemiah knew the state of his people because he listened to them.

Becoming so involved within our personal circles that we grow distant from those not directly connected to our activities can happen quickly. We lead busy lives with sports, meetings, committees, volunteering, and prayer sessions. Our social circles slowly reduce themselves to include only those who are like-minded. Over time, these relational groups tend to become exclusive.

We smile and greet each other at church without pausing and listening because we have one more thing to do before the service. Of course, as soon as the service ends, we have a list of people we must talk to. After getting to as many of those as possible, everyone else is gone. Another successful Sunday? You may have gotten through your list, but at what expense?

If you are not accessible, how will people ever feel comfortable sharing with you? One thing is sure: you will not be approachable if people do not know you, and people will not know you if you cannot take the time to listen and care.

Our church's leadership team is comprised of nine elders. Several months ago, most people would likely have been able to name only five or six of these elders. We began a campaign to increase the visibility of our elders by rotating the benediction each week and including a monthly writeup on varying subjects by each elder in our weekly newsletter.

By intentionally creating more visibility for our leadership team, people began to diffuse their input to multiple elders. Rather than everyone coming only to the chair with their concerns, we created an avenue for multiple contact points and relational availability.

Following Nehemiah's example, we are encouraged to know each other and share concerns. "An intelligent heart acquires knowledge, and the ear of the wise seeks knowledge" (Prov. 18:15). Open your ears to those around you. Take the time to really listen to their hearts. The next time you are eager to get something crossed off your list, intentionally slow yourself down. Start to recognize those you pass by with only a side glance. Are they seeking to talk with you? The knowledge you gain will build trust and allow others' confidence in you to grow.

Assuming that everything is peaceful because you have not heard of any turmoil is dangerous. Cultivate cross-cultural and cross-generational relationships. Steer yourself toward those with whom you may not have much in common. The broader the range of voices you are willing to listen to, the more likely you will hear what is going on—and be able to address it—before anything gets out of control.

Finally, commit to listening without distraction. If listening is particularly challenging for you, find a book or online resource that will help, and then take time to learn.

We often make decisions by relying only upon our own knowledge base. Including others in decisions and bringing them along will engender their support. Leading through turmoil requires a steady support base. Listening and getting to know people with diverse opinions steadies and broadens that base.

Unjust Gains

I bought my first new car when I was twenty-three years old. I worked professionally for over a year and had not saved enough money to pay cash, so I took out a 5-year car loan at 15.5 percent interest. Upon hearing the interest rate, my father offered to loan me the money at 12 percent. I quickly accepted his offer, paid off my original loan, and began paying my father instead.

Several months into this arrangement, I began to feel that this deal was unfair. I knew what the Bible said about not charging interest to your own people, and I grew increasingly bitter each month that I made a payment. Finally, I approached my dad and asked why he charged me such a high interest rate when that was counter to biblical teaching. His response? "Because you agreed to it." (Side note—we renegotiated.)

Usury is defined as "the illegal, unethical, or immoral act of lending money at unreasonably high rates of interest that unfairly enrich the lender." The prohibition against usury was well-known before Nehemiah. The Torah is clear-cut on the subject:

Exodus 22:25 states, "If you lend money to My people, to the poor among you, you are not to act as a creditor to him; you shall not charge him interest."

Leviticus 25:37 is even more explicit concerning our treatment of those who have fallen on hard times:

> *Now in case a countryman of yours becomes poor and his means with regard to you falter, then you are to sustain him, like a stranger or a sojourner, that he may live with you. Do not take usurious interest from him, but revere your God, that your countryman may live with you. You shall not give him your silver at interest, nor your food for gain.*

Nehemiah discovered that a particular group of Jews was employing usury against fellow Jews. One of my favorite verses in this book is when Nehemiah states, "And I consulted with myself" (Neh. 5:7). He did not need to do any research. Nehemiah knew what God's Word said. He knew right from wrong.

Likewise, we need to be willing to boldly confront wrongdoing. When encountering situations that are clearly against God's Word, we are to stand our ground and remind others of what God says about what is going on, even if it means alienating those who believe they are in control but are actually perpetrating the wrong.

The rulers and nobles were exacting money from the Jewish people to fatten their purses. Upon hearing of his people's misfortunes, Nehemiah immediately worked to remedy the situation and restore the ill-gotten gains. After confronting the nobles and rulers with God's rules on usury, each took an oath to return the money.

These leaders responded to Nehemiah's taking them to task

with an "Amen," and then they praised the Lord. Just as Nehemiah did not need fasting or prayer to know what was right, the leaders did not need time to consider. Justice for the people was swift. Everything that had been taken was given back and restored to his people.

Amos 5:24 states, "But let justice roll down like waters and righteousness like an ever-flowing stream." When we know what is right in God's eyes and do it, God's justice flows to His people, allowing them to turn the praise back to Him. Sometimes, the right thing only needs a tiny spark to start the flow.

In Luke 6:34–36, Jesus steps the principle up a notch by saying,

And if you lend to those from whom you expect to receive, what credit is that to you? Even sinners lend to sinners, in order to receive back the same amount. But love your enemies, and do good, and lend, expecting nothing in return; and your reward will be great, and you will be sons of the Most High; for He Himself is kind to ungrateful and evil men. Be merciful, just as your Father is merciful.

Jesus is looking at the condition of our hearts. How we treat each other matters.

While usury may not be a problem within your circles, condition yourself to listen for the words "That is not fair." Often this is when Jesus may ask you to step in to allow God's justice to flow.

Not long ago, during a slight downturn at work, we had a task that would have provided full-time employment for one of our admin staff for a solid month. Everything was set up for her to begin right after she returned from vacation. Instead, her supervisor told her that a newer junior staff member would take on the task. He then cut her hours to half-time since she no longer had enough work to do. He had recently hired this new person and wanted to save face—at the expense of the more-qualified person.

When I heard about it, the immediate injustice was apparent. The fact that the supervisor was unwilling to approach or discuss this with me was also telling. I did not need to hold a meeting to talk about qualifications or workload. Fortunately, there was time to recover and set things right.

We may be afraid to hold people accountable for their actions, not wanting to hurt or offend them. Often those with power or authority over others cause injustices. However, ignoring what we know is unjust may sidestep the real issue that needs to be addressed.

We would do well to grasp this lesson from Nehemiah: our responsibility is to confront situations where unjust or unfair practices are occurring wherever we find them and allow God's justice to flow.

Pull Your Own Weight

Young people, particularly when in high school or deciding on a career, are often asked, "What do you want to do when you grow up?" Often, the question indirectly asks for the worth or value these young adults will bring to society. Rarely are they asked, "Who do you want to be when you grow up?" There is a world of difference between the two questions.

When I was young, I knew beyond a shadow of a doubt that I wanted to be a mom. That was my ultimate goal. I could think of no better way to spend my life than nurturing and caring for a child. I loved my mom and wanted nothing more than to be like her.

What I wanted to do with my life was another question altogether. I loved math and science and (reasonably enough) ended up as an engineer like my father and brother. While engineering was what I wanted to do, it was not who I wanted to be.

During my senior year at college, I gave a speech at a banquet for incoming freshmen. This was for a group of pre-majors in math, engineering, and computer science who were recipients of the same four-year scholarship I had received. I remember telling them to choose something they were passionate about that could satisfy them throughout their life rather than following easy money.

The sense of who we want to be will drive us far more than what we do. In fact, several intentional choices my husband and I made as we raised our children were based on my desire to be a mom, including working part-time for many years to be able to care for my children at home.

While that is not a choice others want or can make, it satisfied a need so deeply embedded in my soul that it carried me through periods of questioning when I saw others being promoted or advanced at work who were less qualified than myself. The occasional revisiting of this decision only strengthened my resolve.

———

The book of Nehemiah clearly talks about what Nehemiah did with his life. He was a cupbearer to the king, a man of prayer, and led the people to rebuild the wall in Jerusalem. Nehemiah was an influential strategist. He became governor of the province. Beyond what he did with his life, Nehemiah 5 reveals the motivation behind his actions—deep faith and humility.

As governor, Nehemiah was entitled to several perks. He

would have been expected to feed and entertain various visiting dignitaries and nearby local rulers and nobles. Nehemiah's table could serve 150 Jews and officials, plus visiting officials from nearby nations. Nehemiah could reasonably expect the people to support his needs as governor.

Yet Nehemiah notes that for twelve years, he and his kinsmen declined the governor's food allowance due to them. He also records that he did not buy up the surrounding land, which would have served to increase his power base, nor did he receive silver taxes for himself from the people.

His rationale for not requiring his allotment was two-fold: the servitude was heavy on his people (Neh. 5:18), and he revered God (Neh. 5:15). At the deepest and most personal level, Nehemiah was a man who did not demand what he was due but lived humbly and loved God, thinking of others before himself. He refused taxes from his people that would have created hardship for them.

First Peter 5:6 encourages us: "Humble yourselves, therefore, under the mighty hand of God, that He may exalt you at the proper time." Strong leaders are commonly known for their humility.

Leaders are often equated with strong, decisive, domineering people with commanding personalities. We are reminded here that leading from a position of humility is the true test of leadership. God honors and exalts those who live genuinely humble lives, allowing those people to be leaders wherever they may be.

Our lifestyle often tells us more about ourselves than we care to admit. Many of us could name one or two visible national Christian leaders with a lavish or flashy lifestyle. Invariably, excuses are offered. The personal jet gets them to places more quickly to preach about Jesus. The sprawling home allows more people to attend fundraisers for the underprivileged. Private drivers permit them to engage in ministry at all times.

Yet these people are often the ones nonbelievers point to as a reason they would never seek to know Jesus. In flaunting their wealth, these people do more harm than good. Their witness does not match someone who is following and becoming more like Jesus.

The question of how much is enough has no easy answer. What is right for one person may not be suitable for another. We should never place ourselves in a position of judging others for what they do or do not have.

Nehemiah did not compare his lifestyle with other rulers or nobles from the surrounding lands. He only commented on how he lived and why. We must be willing to turn an internal spotlight on ourselves and ask for the humility to be able to see clearly. One of the most challenging things you can do is to ask God to humble you at any point you are growing proud—and mean it.

Summary

We are in a war of increasingly competitive worldviews where we must engage in spiritual battle daily. The threat is not simply external. Internally, we are divided by politics, racial injustice, sexuality, and gender issues. Civil discourse degenerates into the need to be correct. Believers fight against believers.

At some point in your life, you will encounter inner turmoil within the community of believers. The relational leadership concepts in this chapter will prepare you to engage and overcome these struggles.

First, create intentional visibility and breadth of contact with those outside your immediate sphere of influence to recognize underlying turmoil more readily. Learn to listen well and create space for conversations. Stand firmly grounded in God's Word, hold others accountable, and always be cognizant of the potential warning flag of someone claiming, "It's not fair."

Be an ambassador for those who cannot speak for themselves by boldly and willingly standing firm for justice and holding others accountable to God's Word. Finally, ensure your lifestyle and possessions reflect a growing dependence upon becoming more like Jesus. Be willing to converse honestly with God about how your life embraces and reflects living humbly before Him.

CONSIDER

As you look at groups of believers on opposite sides of an argument, or when encountering turmoil within your community, what role can you play? How can the relational leadership concepts of listening, standing firm to God's Word, and living in humility help defuse the situation?

PRAYER

Holy Spirit, open my heart and mind to who You have created me to be. Give me clarity into my motivations for everything I do. Help me reflect You more deeply in my life. May my eyes be opened to see others who go unnoticed so I may engage and listen deeply. Give me the boldness to stand firm and hold others accountable to Your Word. But most of all, create in me a clean heart and renew a spirit that allows me to humble myself before You. Amen.

~6~

Personal Attacks

Such things as you are saying have not been done, but you are inventing them in your own mind (Neh. 6:8).

IN THE 1939 VERSION OF THE MOVIE *The Wizard of Oz*, Dorothy, the Scarecrow, and the Tin Man conjure up potential dangers on the road to the Emerald City, repeating, "Lions and Tigers and Bears, oh my!" while steadily advancing along the yellow brick road. Not long after they begin their fearful chant, the Cowardly Lion roars and jumps out at them.

Although the danger was ultimately defused when Dorothy slapped the Cowardly Lion's nose, the attack was real, with a tangible sense of imminent, personal danger.

Nehemiah had already encountered numerous alarming situations, contending with external assaults (chapter 4) and turmoil among his people (chapter 5). Nehemiah's presence in Jerusalem had created powerful enemies. His known enemies, Sanballat, Tobiah, and Geshem, were joined by "the rest of our enemies" (Neh. 6:1). His adversaries were no longer just a few. His enemies resorted to personal attacks to dissuade him from completing the wall.

In engineering, a technique often employed in problem-solving is called "root cause analysis," a method of identifying an underlying cause for a situation. The problem cannot be solved until the deepest underlying cause is determined. Unless the root of the problem is exposed, removing symptoms provides only a temporary reprieve, and the issue will most likely pop up again.

One of the best ways to determine the root cause of a situation is to ask "why" repeatedly until there is no other answer to that question. At that point, you would say that you have established and can now address the root cause.

Asking a couple of simple questions gets to the root cause of the personal attacks. Why did Nehemiah have enemies? Because he was rebuilding the wall. Why did his enemies not want the wall rebuilt? Because it took power away from them. It was less about Nehemiah himself and more about the loss of power by those in control before Nehemiah arrived.

As of follower of Jesus, you can be sure about one thing: at some point in your life, you will be personally attacked. Expect it, be prepared, and search out the root cause for why. Understanding why you are being attacked will help you develop countermeasures. Knowing your mission and staying steadily on your current path are the best defenses against attacks that are meant to frighten you.

Nehemiah dealt with three types of personal attacks: spies within his ranks, lies that discredited him, and betrayal by a trusted advisor. As Solomon states in Ecclesiastes 1:9, "What has been is what will be, and what has been done will be done again; there is nothing new under the sun." All three of these types of attacks are still used against believers today. Let us explore Nehemiah's relational leadership concepts and how to handle each type of attack through a life of perseverance.

Spies

Espionage is no respecter of persons. Governments employ spies to discover military or political secrets of other governments. Corporate espionage entices those willing to be paid to betray company secrets. Although espionage is often handsomely rewarded, it is just as often done out of pride for the spy's country of origin.

As I write this, tonight's headline news announced the arrest of and espionage charges against a former CIA officer. Espionage forms an entire genre of films and books. As a society, we are fascinated with the idea of spying.

Our human nature mentors us in the art of spying from an early age. I am sure I am not alone in overhearing conversations of my siblings to use it against them later or bribing a sibling with the phrase, "I'll tell Mom unless . . ." In fourth grade, I even hid in my best friend's closet to watch her boyfriend give her a kiss so we could tease him later. (Lord, forgive us.)

To rationalize our spying, we may even believe that the end justifies the means. But espionage is a traitorous act. Embedded in its definition is the intent to deceive. Personal reasons can never justify the action, regardless of how noble we believe a cause to be.

Nehemiah 6 begins with all breaches in the wall having been closed. The only thing left to do was hang doors in the open gates. Nehemiah's enemies were nervous. Completion of the wall meant a loss of power. Finishing the gates would culminate in their loss of control. Each day, the completion of the gates was closer. It became important to stop Nehemiah before it was too late.

They first employed espionage to try to overthrow Nehemiah.

The first plan was hatched by Sanballat and Geshem. Three times they requested to meet directly with Nehemiah. They offered to meet on an open plain, which gave the perception of safety. Yet each time, he made excuses.

The excuse, "Why should the work stop?" (Neh. 6:3), made no sense. He was just one man. Would it really have impeded the work for him to meet them? Nehemiah's knowledge that they intended to harm him is what kept him safe. He knew that "they were planning to harm me." (Neh. 6:2).

Tobiah's turn was next by planting spies within Nehemiah's own court. Many of the nobles of Judah were bound by oath to Tobiah due to a marriage treaty. Tobiah had them in his back pocket. These nobles took turns reporting Tobiah's good deeds to Nehemiah while also secretly recording Nehemiah's words for Tobiah, who used them to write threatening letters to Nehemiah.

Nehemiah did not seek to root out and displace these spies. He realized that they would only be replaced by others. At least with these, he knew with whom he was dealing!

The saying, "Hold your friends close and your enemies closer," is attributed to Michael Corleone in *The Godfather, Part II*. However, many believe it may have originated with Kabir Das, a famous fifteenth-century Indian mystic poet. The principle is thought-provoking. Keeping your enemies close allows you to be in lockstep with them, think on their terms, and potentially undermine their plans. It also provides an opportunity for transformation.

At one point in my career, I worked with a woman who did everything she could to sabotage my advancement. She put on a friendly face and a saccharine sweet smile whenever we met, but behind the scenes, she was nasty, demeaning, and derogatory about me to everyone she knew. Knowing what she was doing but unable to defend myself, I began applying this concept to our interactions.

I held her closer than a friend. I knew her comings and goings and asked about her personal life and hoped-for career growth. I made excuses to swing by her office unexpectedly. I went to lunch and had more coffees with her than I can count.

Somewhere along the way, a transformation began. We never became friends, but respect was established. The spying and reporting she was doing were no longer effective. Her power had been neutralized.

In Galatians 2, Paul recounts his return to Jerusalem with Barnabas and Titus. He speaks of those trying to "spy out the liberty which we have in Christ Jesus" (Gal. 2:4) to bring new Gentile converts back into bondage regarding circumcision. His next statement is clear and decisive: "But we did not yield in subjection to them for even an hour, so that the truth of the gospel might remain with you" (Gal. 2:5). Paul stood firm in the face of enemies who were trying to undermine the work of the gospel.

Keep Paul's words in mind and do not yield. As attacks come, as spies spread rumors or seek to undermine your authority, hold fast. Do not believe that just because you serve God, enemies will not be trying to personally undermine you, your leadership, or someone on your team. You may never know their rationale, but that does not matter. You are simply called to stand firm.

Lies

Synonyms of the word "lies" include libel, deceit, slander, defamation, falsehood, guile, distortion, misrepresentation, and malicious gossip. Each word has a slight nuance that makes it different from the others. Looking at this list, we see nothing positive about the act of lying. We may try to justify it by saying we are trying to protect another's feelings, but simply put, lying is an intent to deceive or distort the truth.

A witness taking the stand in court will be asked to promise that what they are about to say is "the truth, the whole truth, and nothing but the truth." Being guilty of lying under oath includes stiff penalties or jail time. The term "lie" has so many subtle meanings that the intent is for all three parts of this oath to focus on a slightly different facet of truth, trying to eliminate any possibility of lying or deception by the witness.

We are accountable for our words. Throughout the Bible, we are admonished not to lie. From Genesis through Revelation, there are almost 300 verses about lying. Proverbs 12:22 states, "Lying lips are an abomination to the Lord." Almost an entire chapter of James is devoted to the harsh condemnation of our words: "But no one can tame the tongue; it is a restless evil and full of deadly poison. With it we bless our Lord and Father; and with it we curse men, who have been made in the likeness of God" (James 3:8–9).

Nehemiah refused to meet with his enemies four times. The fifth time, Nehemiah received an open letter from Sanballat, which (regardless of the contents) was a concern. A letter must pass through multiple hands to reach its intended recipient. Typically, private communications were sealed to protect the contents from being read by others.

Sanballat wanted to spread lies as quickly as possible, and the contents of an unsealed letter would most likely be read as it passed through each courier's hands before being given to Nehemiah. He was hopeful that the contents of the letter would cause rumors to swirl, forcing Nehemiah to step back from power in disgrace.

Sanballat went for the big lie. Implying that he was only repeating what a known truth was, he stated, "It is reported among the nations" (Neh. 6:6) that Nehemiah had appointed prophets to anoint himself as king in place of King Artaxerxes.

Regardless of how far this rumor had already spread, Nehemiah knew it was not the truth, nor did he take the lie as an attack only against himself. He noted that his enemies were trying to frighten them to cause the work to stop. It was an attack on his entire leadership team. His response? "But now, O God, strengthen my hands" (Neh. 6:9). He again reverted to the fact that God had given him this task, and therefore nothing man tried would turn him aside from completing it.

A critical component of leading through personal attacks is to know the purpose to which God has called you and then living in that until He releases you.

God was clear when He called me to be our church chair. I had been praying about it for several weeks without clear direction. One Sunday, as our lead pastor was preaching, I heard God clearly challenging me with the question, "If I ask you to do something, are you going to say no?" I said, "Of course not, Lord." He asked again. I repeated my response.

I did not relate this in any way to my search for an answer about the chair position. He asked a third time with a slightly different inflection, "If I ask you to do something, are you *really* going to say no?" It immediately dawned on me that He was asking me to accept the role of chair. As the service concluded, I went to the lead pastor and took the chair position.

Knowing the clarity of that call was instrumental in ensuring I remained where God wanted me through the season in which He needed me in that position. Several times I questioned whether I should step down.

One of our associate pastors gave me words that carried me through these times of questioning: If God has called you, only God can un-call you. I knew God had called me, so I remained in that position through extremely tough circumstances until it was clear that God had released me.

Ephesians encourages us to know our calling: "I pray that the eyes of your heart may be enlightened, so that you may know what is the hope of His calling" (Eph. 1:18). We are each called to a specific ministry at a particular time. Do not be discouraged by rumors.

You may need to deal with outright lies, but do not let them sway you from your work. To the extent God has given you clarity in your mission, walk into that work with boldness, expecting Him to protect and carry you until you are uncalled.

Betrayal

Years ago, Michael Card and John Michael Talbot recorded the song "Why," which focuses on the crucifixion of Jesus. While the music is haunting and each verse poignant, the chorus gets to the heart of why a betrayal can hurt us so profoundly. It talks about how only a friend can betray a friend while others have nothing to attain, and only a friend can cause us deep pain. The closer we allow someone to come to us emotionally, the more we trust them. The more we trust them, the more pain they can inflict.

Our world is filled with broken relationships, broken marriages, and broken people. At times, brokenness comes through no fault of our own. We may be doing everything we can to hold things together, but the brokenness comes anyway.

If our hope is in ourselves, we remain broken. Why do humans continue to trust others? Indeed, if life has taught us anything, it is that allowing people to get close to us can set us up for hurt.

Over the last fifty years, the divorce rate in the U.S. has been on the rise. Nearly half of all marriages end in divorce. For second marriages, the statistics are even worse, with a divorce rate closer to 60 percent. While studies show that the divorce rate has been falling recently, that is not necessarily good news, as over the last twenty years, cohabitation has risen to nearly 15 percent.

Obviously, no one entering a marriage hopes for a divorce. Although some couples part amicably, bitterness frequently develops between the partners that may take years to overcome.

In an article in *Psychology Today* entitled "Why Do People Divorce" (Dr. Ann Gold Buschol, Ph.D., Feb 2020), Dr. Buschol describes the difficulties in pinpointing the exact cause of a divorce. One statement stands out in the article: "In my work with clients, I have seen that 'betrayal' underlies most of the reasons given." Betrayal is the key to many broken relationships.

Every relationship contains expectations. Relationships are founded upon trust. When trust is broken, a connection will begin to erode unless intentional efforts are made to reestablish or rebuild trust. Why does someone choose to betray another? There is no single, solitary reason. Every broken relationship will vary in the "why."

Some betrayals are intentional, as was the case for Nehemiah. Nehemiah had gone to the home of a friend.

During the evening, the threats he had received came up, and his friend began to pressure him to hide in the temple with his family so they would not be killed. Rather than supporting and providing strength to him, he basically asked Nehemiah to be a coward and protect himself—at the expense of his people.

Only then did Nehemiah realize his friend has been hired by Tobiah and Sanballat to betray him and encourage actions "so that they might have an evil report in order that they could reproach me" (Neh. 6:13). The NIV states, ". . . then they would give me a bad name to discredit me."

I cannot imagine the feelings that must have accompanied this betrayal. With everything Nehemiah had already encountered with spies and lies by his enemies, the betrayal by his friend would have been devastating. He could no longer trust the motives of friends within his own inner circle.

Nehemiah responded in a way that is becoming familiar. While acknowledging the betrayal, he did not act or react in anger. We have repeatedly seen him turn situations like this over to God to handle with the simple words, "Remember, O my God . . ." He had implicit trust that at the right time, God would remember the actions of others and deal with them accordingly.

Romans 12:9 (NLT) reminds us, "Dear friends, never take revenge. Leave that to the righteous anger of God. For the Scriptures say, 'I will take revenge; I will pay them back,' says the Lord." Nehemiah exemplified this verse by his response.

———

Overcoming betrayal is difficult. Months after someone left our leadership team at church, I learned of several acts of backstabbing, specifically against me as the church Chair. It hurt deeply. I was oblivious to these acts and genuinely believed our relationship was built on mutual respect and trust.

What made this so difficult was that I could no longer confront or reconcile with this person because this person was gone. In hindsight, that is where God precisely wanted me to be: unable to do anything about it.

I went through a period of outrage before I was finally able to release my anger and hurt. Like Nehemiah, I finally said, "Remember, O My God ..." And I let it go. I trusted that Jesus would take care of it for me someday.

I have found that betrayal does not have levels of hurt. Any degree of it is painful. We do not intend to live in distrust of others, but we recognize that every person stands a chance of being betrayed at some point. For leaders, the stakes seem higher because others are closely watching how they respond.

If we desire to become more like Jesus, we need to let Him take care of situations that are His to handle in the first place. We must be willing to do nothing when betrayed. Those words are easier to say than to do, but inaction is imperative to keep our hearts from becoming hardened and to allow us to continue to trust others.

SUMMARY

Despite the obstacles and attacks that Nehemiah and his people endured, the wall around Jerusalem was completed. The response of those who had tried to cause the project to fail is a powerful testimony to God. The enemies and all the nations surrounding Jerusalem, "lost their confidence, for they recognized that this work had been accomplished with the help of our God" (Neh. 6:16).

When God gives you a task, take heart. You will encounter difficulties. Knowing God's direction does not mean the sailing will always be smooth. No one enjoys dealing with personal attacks, but applying the relational leadership concepts within this chapter will allow you to hone your leadership skills to overcome attacks when they arise. The key to all these is in this verse: "Be strong in the Lord and in the strength of His might" (Eph. 6:10).

When spies spread rumors or seek to undermine your authority, stand firm. Do not be swayed by lies but remain on the path He has called you until you are released. Finally, in situations of betrayal, rely on and trust Jesus to set things right someday.

CONSIDER

At some point in your life, you may experience spying, lying, or betrayal by someone close to you. We have explored how to stand firm in the face of rumors, hold fast to the call Jesus has given, and allow Him to handle betrayal. Can these actions counter the hurt?

PRAYER

God of Hosts, may the words "Remember, O Lord God" be my first words when I am personally attacked. Keep me from taking matters into my own hands. May I always be willing to leave the ending to You. I ask for wisdom to see the schemes of others that are counter to what You have called me to do. Help me to stand firm and lead from a position of reliance on You. Where trust is broken, may I be the one to begin rebuilding, always pointing to Jesus as my example. Amen.

~7~

New Beginnings

Then my God put it into my heart to assemble the nobles, the officials, and the people to be enrolled by genealogies (Neh. 7:5).

THE UNITED STATES HAS COUNTED ITS PEOPLE every decade since 1790. Broadly defined, the census counts all people dwelling in the United States regardless of citizenship status, race, or age. Overseas residents working for the federal government and their dependents are also included. Actual enumeration is used rather than statistical sampling techniques, meaning every attempt is made to obtain a personal and verifiable count.

The primary purpose of the census is to reapportion the number of persons assigned by state to the House of Representatives. Allocation of federal funding in many programs is based on the census count, which is why including young children and the homeless is essential. The flow of funds for transportation and infrastructure, military and disaster response planning, and economic analysis rely upon the census and its accuracy.

The census is also often used as a political tool, as is seen with the current power play in potential statehood for the District of Columbia. With D.C. residents trending toward more substantial alignment with the Democratic party, a Republican-controlled White House would not want additional Democrats added to the roster in the House of Representatives.

———

Back in Nehemiah, the wall and gates around Jerusalem have been completed. We can almost sense Nehemiah's mind spinning as he considers his next steps. Even though the wall is built, his task is far from complete. In Nehemiah 7, the process of creating a stable local government begins.

Once again, we see Nehemiah's deep and underlying reliance on the Lord. He states, "Then, my God put it into my heart ..." He did not start a flurry of programs or activities to fill the time used to build the wall. Instead, he again returns to his source, seeking God's wisdom and guidance.

Seeking God's direction must always be the first step. Multiple passages throughout the Bible provide stern warnings against relying on our own wisdom. "The shepherds of my people have lost their senses. They no longer seek wisdom from the Lord. Therefore, they fail completely, and their flocks are scattered" (Jer. 10:21 NLT).

As Nehemiah begins to normalize the period following the wall's completion, he relies on God for each step in the process. The first thing Nehemiah hears from God is that he is to care for and bind his people together by establishing robust local governance.

Chapter 7 provides us with three concepts employed by Nehemiah within the realm of spiritual leadership that focuses on a life of waiting. First, we must be willing to wait on Jesus to provide direction when one task ends and the next has not yet begun. Secondly, we will look at the valuable concept of having an intimate knowledge of those around us, helping them find a place of belonging. Finally, and most critically, we are to develop ways of grafting those outside our fellowship into our communities.

Now What?

I vividly remember a Christmas morning when I was about ten. My brother, sister, and I ran into our living room to open our presents. I tore through mine as quickly as possible, barely looking at each. And then, I just sat there among my gifts. I felt empty. The elation I had felt just moments before had shifted completely. The previous joy felt hollow.

I wish this was an isolated incident, but it was not. I recall going to the Rose Bowl in college and, even while cheering as the University of Washington Huskies won, wondering about the hollowness of the victory. What else is there when you have already received, won, or completed the ultimate? What happens when the thrill wears off?

The human heart is not wired to be satisfied with the temporal. Isaiah 55:2 asks, "Why do you spend money for what is not bread and your wages for what does not satisfy?" Ecclesiastes chronicles Solomon, the wealthiest man in the world at the time, as he strives to find something to satisfy his innermost needs. He denies himself nothing yet concludes after each successive try that it is meaningless. It is like striving after the wind, searching for what cannot be captured.

God never intended for us to be content with what the world offers. Wealth, power, position, and fame are all empty. The ache He has placed in our hearts can be satisfied with nothing less than Himself. No wonder we feel the hollowness of success. It is an imposter.

Nehemiah had just completed what could easily be called one of the most wildly successful projects ever envisioned. In less than two months, the entire wall around Jerusalem had been rebuilt despite numerous sabotage attempts. We can well imagine Nehemiah's feelings as he looked at all that had been done and wondered, *Now what?*

Here again, we are given a glimpse of the genius of Nehemiah. He knows that completing the wall does not mean his work is done. He does not sit back and rest. He continued exhibiting his leadership by establishing a management and protection framework for the people.

Nehemiah ensured that the essential functions of society resumed. He assigned a rotation of gatekeepers to each portal to manage the comings and goings of the city. Nehemiah appointed singers and Levites to ensure the religious festivities were reinstated. He placed people he trusted, his brother and the commander of the fortress, in charge of Jerusalem. Basically, he established a local government to take over the day-to-day management of the city.

Nehemiah also understood that his enemies had gone nowhere even though the wall was completed. He implemented policies that ensured the continued protection of his people. The gates were only opened after the sun had risen high to ensure good visibility for the gatekeepers and prevent enemies from advancing while the light was poor. Additionally, guards were appointed to supplement the defense provided by the wall.

When we complete a project, it can be tempting to feel like we deserve a break, that we should be able to have a bit of time off, or we may jump right into the next thing, staying busy to keep the feeling of hollowness away. Stepping into another program or activity that needs to be done can be too straight-forward without considering if that is where God is calling us next.

We must consciously step back to allow God time to speak into our hearts. When you experience a "what's next?" moment, resist the temptation to start a list of outstanding tasks. This is not the time to create a brainstorming list. Instead, take time to wait on God.

Psalm 46:10 states, "Cease striving and know that I am God." Footnotes further define "cease striving" as "let go" or "relax." Other versions, including the NIV say, "Be still." Regardless of the version, the intent is the same.

We must stop trying to figure out what is next for our lives on our own and simply wait for God to speak. We can get hung up on needing to be in motion and active. Never forget that busyness can interfere with being able to hear God clearly.

I think of the well-known story of Jesus going to dinner at Lazarus' home. Lazarus' sister, Martha, is frustrated that Jesus is not telling her sister, Mary, to help with the preparations. Instead, Mary is sitting and listening to Jesus. Yet Jesus answers that Mary has chosen the better path. She has ceased striving and is just waiting to hear Jesus.

May Mary be our role model when we are tempted to jump into the next thing (and there is always a next thing). We need to learn to take the time to be silent and listen for Jesus to direct our next steps. Grab hold of the opportunity presented with the question, "Now what?" as a chance to realign your team and yourself with God's leading.

Roll Call

Growing up as an Episcopalian, I became familiar with

their governance model. As a child, speaking about the House of Bishops or the Diocesan Convention around the dinner table was not uncommon. I knew our congregation was at the lowest point in this model, receiving oversight and care from those specifically trained and commissioned to oversee our local parish. While there was certainly room for local decisions, our identity was to remain aligned with the canons of the Episcopal church.

The governance of my upbringing greatly contrasts to the governance of the church we now attend, where the organizational structure is flipped. The congregation provides the ultimate governing authority for all direction and decisions of our church, with ultimate denominational polity maintained through an annual meeting of delegates from each participant congregation.

For me, this reversal brought welcome freedom that allowed me a level of voice in our congregation that resonated well with my spirit. Congregationally led, our church ensures that decisions and direction capture the discerned position of all members, with meetings carefully orchestrated to ensure we have a quorum before any discussion or voting occurs. Representation is key to the congregational policy.

Membership is highly encouraged, with multiple opportunities offered throughout the year to allow all who want to be involved in our governance to do so. Beyond this, we seek opportunities to get to know our people. Every year, we go through our membership lists to ensure they are accurate. The representation needed for our congregational meetings relies upon good stewardship of our people.

God called Nehemiah to perform a census. It had been

over seventy years since almost ten thousand people were relocated to Babylon after the fall of Jerusalem to King Nebuchadnezzar. Throughout their exile, the Jewish people carefully preserved their cultural identity, continuing their religious practices and remaining united in their faith in Yahweh. The census gave Nehemiah a chance to learn the names and stories of his people.

Nehemiah 7 lists those who returned from exile by name, each of whom was included in Nehemiah's census. All men, sons, priests, Levites, singers, gatekeepers, and temple servants were counted. Family groups ranged from 42 to 3,930, excluding servants. Even the horses, mules, camels, and donkeys were part of the census!

The assembly comprised of 42,360 men, four times the size of the group that left. While women were not included, you can imagine how the numbers would have swelled had women and servants been included. Nehemiah 7 also consists of a listing of financial contributions to the rebuilding effort.

We are not given the specific purpose of the census; however, with Nehemiah's previous concerns of usury and over-taxation, these counts would have ensured appropriate taxation, like how our current-day census determines the support provided by the federal government to those in need.

An intangible benefit of a census that is difficult to define deals with identity. In the first chapter of this book, we looked at the importance of understanding our identity as Jesus' followers. However, becoming a member of a specific people group, or being counted as part of that group, provides an almost unquantifiable benefit—a sense of belonging.

When I first moved to Massachusetts, my husband and I

were already engaged. Although he was attending the local Episcopal church, we decided to find our own church to attend as a couple. We had what was called "church row" in town—a street with seven churches (and a synagogue) in less than a one-mile stretch.

We would try a new church weekly, looking for the perfect fit. Of course, finding the ideal church was compounded by beginning our search in the summer months when many congregations had low attendance or guest preachers.

Our journey ended, and we began regularly visiting "our" church. This continued year after year. Through marriage and the birth of two children, we kept going back. For twelve years, we kept attending. Occasionally, someone would ask why we did not become members.

My answer was typically the same, "Why should we?" We were already fully engaged in the life of our church. We taught Sunday School and Bible studies, read Scripture, volunteered, and tithed. I was even a member of the "carpet committee," one of the most challenging ones I have ever served!

Twelve years later (and just months before moving back to Washington state), God prompted us to become members. We dutifully took the classes and joined. I never expected what would happen. I did not just become a member; I now belonged. The sense of family and integration with these people I had learned to love over the years was one of the most fulfilling things I had ever experienced.

Why had I not joined years before? Describing the completeness that I felt is almost impossible. The meaning of belonging sank in deeply. Paul says, "So then you are no longer strangers and aliens, but you are fellow citizens with the saints, and are of God's household" (Eph 2:19).

One of the first and foremost responsibilities of a leader is stewardship. If you oversee or have charge over anyone else, whether as a mother or a CEO, you are the leader. Your stewardship includes helping others understand the importance of belonging and tapping into a place where they can best explore what that means. Something as simple as connecting to a church may drastically change how they view what it means to be part of God's family.

Grafted In

The practice of horticulture as a science separate from agriculture dates from the Middle Ages in Europe. While having many similarities, horticulture includes the specialized grafting method, a technique by which the tissues of two (or more) plants are blended to produce a separate and unique plant. Grafting includes creating new varietals, developing drought or disease resistance, repairing a plant, or easing propagation.

Here are some grafting basics. First, a primary base plant is chosen. This base plant, the rootstock, is the one to which the second plant will be grafted. The rootstock must be healthy, well-rooted, and disease resistant.

Several techniques are employed for grafting the smaller plant, the scion, onto the rootstock; however, one of the more common methods includes sharpening the end of the scion and pushing it several inches directly into the stem or trunk of the rootstock. The two plants are then bound together and nurtured until the graft takes.

For grafting to work, the plants must be closely related. Once grafted, the individual plants are no longer identifiable; they are joined by their very tissues to create something new.

Once the concept of grafting is understood, the biblical use

of the term becomes clear. Grafting signifies the joining together
of separate groups to become one unified body. One of the most
notable passages on grafting is Romans 11:17-25, which explains
how gentiles are grafted into the body of Christ.

The base rootstock is the Jewish believers. In the book of
Romans, they are symbolized by an olive tree. God breaks off
dead branches of unbelief and grafts a wild olive tree, the gentiles, onto the more robust body. The gentiles "... became par-
takers with them of the root and fatness of the olive tree"
(Rom. 11:17).

As the census in Nehemiah 7 was being conducted, two
groups of people could not provide documentation of their
Jewish identity. Somewhere along the way, they had lost their
ancestral records and could not prove who they were.
Nehemiah dealt with each group differently. He didn't want
to exclude anyone, so the first group was counted in the census
by name, even though they could not provide backup.

The second group were priests, who were not allowed to
retain their status. Nehemiah referred to them as "unclean and
excluded from the priesthood" (Neh. 7:64). Priests cared for
the temple and guided the people in the law and worship of
God. This group was to only include those who were truly
qualified, not only for societal equity reasons but so that none
would enter the presence of Yahweh unless it was lawful for
them to do so.

Nehemiah reveres God so profoundly that he will not
allow these people to continue functioning as priests unless
they can prove their eligibility. Again, wanting to exclude no
one, Nehemiah provides a way for grafting them back into the
priesthood: they will be allowed to reintegrate upon declara-

tion by a high priest. In the meantime, they must remain outside the priestly group.

––––––––––

An example of corporate grafting is through a Merger and
Acquisition (M&A). I have been on both sides of an M&A,
one where my firm was acquired and one where my firm
merged with another. Neither M&A went particularly well. In
the first M&A, I worked for almost ten years for a smaller
national firm in Boston when we merged with a more prominent international engineering firm. Almost everything was
done incorrectly, from numerous minor changes to the firm's
name to a lack of leadership and education of employees for
the processes and procedures being retained. It was a chaotic
period, and many left.

In the second case, the primary growth mechanism for the
firm was through M&As. The biggest issue was the lack of
integration. The old firm names were often retained, with
people referring to themselves as employees of the acquired
firm even years later. Additionally, the acquired firms often had
management processes that reflected a smaller firm mentality.
As the parent company grew, the expectation was that we
would take on larger projects based on the sheer number of
people available, even though no processes were updated to
support this expectation.

The takeaway from both examples is that an integration
team is critical for the success of any M&A. As one firm is
grafted into the other, specialized oversight is needed to ensure
the grafting is successful. Someone in the parent firm must be
willing to teach and train the new firm to avoid the loss of staff
and build rapport and excitement for the new entity. This task
is not easy, but it can be done.

Mergers are not uncommon within the church. Two smaller congregations may join to provide more resources and energy to a shared vision or ministry. Or depending on location, a larger church may acquire a smaller church to begin ministry in a new area. Each merger invariably needs an integration team that works with both congregations to assist during the transition period.

However, the critical point for this chapter is that each of us in the Christian community ought to look for ways to graft in those outside our faith. Spiritual leadership includes considering others as potential "scions" who might create or produce a new kind of fruit within our fellowship. Grafting others into our communities allows their unique talents and giftings to take us somewhere not yet imagined.

We must guard against wanting new people to blend into the way things have always been done. Each of us has a role in an integration team that encourages the grafting of others into our fellowship.

SUMMARY

The concepts in this chapter will develop your ability to spiritually lead through new beginnings. Each idea was explicitly written with you in mind so you can confidently approach each transition you encounter throughout your life or ministry.

When your current calling or task is complete, it will be time to step into something new. This may come with a unique calling or a calling that changes over time. Recognize that this may take time. Be willing to step back and wait until God is clear in His call. Any steps you take that are done on your own effort are fruitless.

As you wait, seek to know those around you more deeply. As a steward of those you oversee, you have a responsibility to help them find their place of belonging, letting them potentially bring new ways of doing things to life.

Finally, understand that you are on a never-ending integration team. Do not require others to be *folded* into an existing organism. Instead, allow them to be *grafted* in. Jesus offers an immediate grafting into His family. Look to those both within and without your circles of influence for those who need Jesus.

CONSIDER

Spiritual leadership extends beyond your current role and prepares you for a future calling. As you make this transition, do the concepts included in this chapter of waiting on direction from God, finding a place of belonging, and grafting others into your fellowship fit? If not, what is missing?

PRAYER

Mighty Lord, strengthen me to step back and abide in You, waiting for Your direction before charging ahead into each new calling. Open my mind to find ways to help others understand the meaning of true belonging. May I take the time to really know those around me, and may they never just be a number. Give me the wisdom to reach out to those different from me and help them graft into my existing fellowship groups. Amen.

∼8∼

God's Word

*And they read from the book, from the law of God, translating
to give the sense so that they understood the reading* (Neh. 8:8).

I AM AN AVID READER. With a strong imagination, I often feel
as if I am living the storyline of my books. Putting a book
down is difficult, even when I know I may only get a few hours
of sleep. I am compelled to keep going, typically telling myself,
"Just one more chapter."

The alternative is not much better because even if I put the
book down, my mind can be so preoccupied that I have no
peace until I pick it up and finish. Although this happens primarily with fictional stories, nonfiction can be as compelling,
depending on the author.

In Nehemiah 8, we are introduced to Ezra, one of
Nehemiah's contemporaries. Ezra had also been sent to
Jerusalem by King Artaxerxes to rebuild Solomon's temple.
Arriving before Nehemiah, he presumably lived in Jerusalem
when the wall was rebuilt.

Ezra was both a scribe and a priest, a direct descendant of
Moses' brother, Aaron. He was one of the leaders when the
people returned from exile in Babylon, and it was under Ezra's
leadership that the Great Assembly, a forerunner of the

Sanhedrin, was created. He was considered an expert concerning matters of Mosaic Law.

Nehemiah knew that although the people had maintained their cultural identity and belief in Yahweh throughout their exile, at this point, their faith was primarily superficial. Ezra was tasked with reestablishing the connection between the people and the law of Moses.

I have several family members who would say with absolute conviction that they are Christians. They grew up in church, attend once or twice a year, and say they believe in God. Are they Christians?

While church attendance is not required to be a Christian, it can be a good indicator. However, the lack of fruit in their lives is much more telling. Often nothing indicates anything remotely resembling a living faith in Jesus. Theirs is a faith of words, not the heart.

———

Nehemiah 8 teaches several spiritual leadership principles for bringing others into a living faith. Ezra began his task by reading the Law to the people. Just as I often cannot put down a good book, the people could not get enough. Hearing Ezra's words, they bowed low and worshipped God, soaking in as much as possible.

The leadership concepts in this chapter focus on a life of study. We begin with spending time in God's Word as a stepping-stone to a deepening faith. Secondly, as we get to know His heart more intimately, we are led to the place where our understanding of who we are in comparison to God's holiness causes us to grieve over our sins.

Finally, knowing that God does not leave us broken but lifts us up, we learn the concept of rejoicing in His grace as we embrace change. Jeremiah 29:13 reminds us, "And you will seek Me and find Me, when you search for Me with all your heart."

Know His Word

My son and I have completely different learning styles. One of my son's biggest frustrations with me is when he tries to teach me a new board game. He wants to start playing and have me absorb the game by watching and participating.

I like to know the rules first, as I believe they are crucial to strategizing and moving effectively. Being introduced to rules as I need them is endlessly vexing to me, and I often wonder if rules are being made up as we go along! On the other side, having to teach me rules that will not make sense until I understand the gist of the game is hugely aggravating to my son.

Humans have multiple styles of learning. Some learn best through hands-on experiences (kinesthetic learners), others prefer to read (visualizers), and still others lean toward listening to instructions (auditory). While these three modes are considered basic, numerous alternate models also exist.

The numerous varieties point to the complexity of pinpointing exactly how the human mind functions. One of the intriguing facets of trying to identify the learning style of someone else is that they can change over time. Additionally, the distinctions between different types can become blurred with age. What worked best for you at one point in your life may no longer be accurate.

During Nehemiah's time, most people's primary form of learning was auditory. As a scribe, Ezra was in a small, unique class of people who could read and write. As Nehemiah realizes that his people do not know or understand the law of Moses, he arranges a time for them to learn.

Ezra gathered all the men and women to the square by the Water Gate, and he began reading the Law to them. On the platform with Ezra were thirteen men, possibly to take turns reading from the Law or possibly to divide the people into more manageable groups. The Levites and thirteen other men were also on the platform to translate and explain what was being read.

Nehemiah did not want this to be just another exercise in hearing the Law. He did everything possible to ensure that the people also understood what they were hearing. He deeply desired that the people would come to know God's Word and become His people—not just in name but in their hearts.

Ezra read from "early morning until midday" (Neh. 8:3), during which time the people stood. However, before he began reading, Ezra blessed God, and the people lifted their hands and voices and shouted, "Amen, Amen!" They bowed low and worshiped the Lord with their faces to the ground (Neh. 8:6). They began with worship!

This mimics many church services today. Have you ever wondered why services often begin with a time of praise and worship? As we worship, something in the human spirit becomes open, soft, and available to God. We become more receptive to preaching and teaching when we have spent time praising and worshiping our Lord.

Once the praise was complete, the people were ready to hear the words of the Law. In addition to reading the Law to the entire crowd, Ezra met with a smaller group the next day. This group included the heads of households, priests, and

Levites, allowing them to "gain insight into the words of the Law" (Neh. 8:13).

Even today, it is not uncommon for more in-depth learning or discussion sessions to be held after a sermon or in a study group during the week. Nehemiah did not want this to be a one-time reading. By bringing together a select group of people to study what they heard the previous day, he was helping the Word become deeply rooted in these people's lives.

Personality assessments are popular tools for interviewing potential new staff. The first time I took a Myers-Briggs assessment, I was a young engineer taking a six-week evening leadership class. I was utterly amazed! How could a simple test so accurately identify my personality traits? Even more impressive was the realization that approaching others in a way that best suited their personality would make all the difference in how we worked together.

Multiple personality tests are available online. Our denomination typically uses the Enneagram Personality Test from the Enneagram Institute. Sometimes we select a book on leadership to work through together, applying its principles as needed. Yet when we dive into God's Word together, we find we grow the most.

Leading well includes utilizing all available tools to better understand how to best work together. This includes knowing the learning styles of everyone with whom we work or engage regularly. Knowing how others function, how they learn, and how to best relate to them will allow you to serve in a way that honors God.

As the Israelites listened to the Law, they believed, "The law of the Lord is perfect, restoring the soul; the testimony of the Lord is sure, making wise the simple. The precepts of the Lord are right, rejoicing the heart; the commandment of the Lord is pure, enlightening the eyes" (Ps. 119:7–8).

Remembering why you are involved in any group is of utmost importance. It is easy to get so focused on activities or business that you forget the critical importance of continuing to strengthen your relationship with Jesus. Activities should never take precedence over growing in your knowledge of Him.

How genuine is your commitment to studying and learning the Word of God? As you focus first and foremost on deepening your knowledge of His Word, others will see and desire to know His Word more intimately too.

Grieve Your Sin

Each person's grief is unique. People go through seven recognized grief stages when dealing with the loss of a loved one: shock, denial, anger, bargaining, depression, testing, and acceptance. The time someone spends in any stage will often depend on the strength of the relationship between that person and the deceased.

My mother was diagnosed with an inoperable, malignant brain tumor in her mid-eighties. We brought her home from the hospital and spent precious time talking, singing, praying, and saying everything that needed to be said. She even had the opportunity to speak blessings and love over each grandchild. We held hands and prayed over her as she passed. Even though her death was anticipated, we were immediately in the throes of intense grief.

What was unanticipated was the death of my father only forty days later. There were no gentle goodbyes. No prayers, no singing, no laughter. Death was hard, cold, and unforgiving. The grief of losing both parents in such proximity was completely overwhelming. I had already gone through several stages of grief before my mother's death, but I entered deep, numbing shock with my dad's passing.

While grief is often triggered by the experience of loss, death is not the only cause. I was surprised at the people's response when Ezra read the law of Moses: "For all the people were weeping when they heard the words of the Law" (Neh. 8:9). The Levites enjoined the people to "not be grieved" (Neh. 8:10–11). What triggered such an unanticipated, intense reaction? Throughout the morning, the people had gone from worshiping and praising God to a state of profound grief.

I believe the most logical explanation is provided in Hebrews 4:12: "For the word of God is living and active and sharper than any two-edged sword, and piercing as far as the division of soul and spirit, of both joints and marrow, and able to judge the thoughts and intentions of the heart." The people's hearts had been readied to hear from God through a powerful time of worship.

As the Law of Moses was read, the difference between how they had been living and how God intended them to live became clear. They saw how far short their lifestyles were from what was intended by Yahweh. They grieved the loss of not walking with God for so many years. They suffered the loss of not knowing they were walking in sin. They regretted how far away their current lifestyle was from living according to His Word.

Each of these facets of grief is still relevant today. In fact, they are often at the heart of repentance for both nonbelievers and believers. Take a deep look at your lifestyle. Do you live a life that genuinely follows Jesus, or are you a Christian in name or heritage only? We have been called to follow Jesus. Anything less should cause us to repent and grieve.

Romans 3:23 reminds us that "all have sinned and fall short of the glory of God." This includes Christians. Never think that you are immune to sin because you are a Christian or the grief and repentance that should come as your heart yields more and more to Him.

In Nehemiah 1, we were called to pray, fast, and repent for the sins of others. Now, however, the repentance we encounter is personal. Although elicited by the corporate reading of the Law, the people here were grieving over their individual participation in a lifestyle that did not honor Yahweh. The repentance had reached their hearts.

Evangelical churches often emphasize salvation more than confession and repentance, with many mainstream churches leaning into the lie that preaching should focus exclusively on discipleship and spiritual growth. They are concerned that people may leave if the focus on sin is too frequent. The words sin and repentance make people uncomfortable, and isn't it the church's job to keep people coming back so they can hear the good news about Jesus?

Several years ago, I was laid prostrate on the floor of my living room by the Holy Spirit. Our church had been called into a time of repentance. After bringing my vision to our lead pastor, we took it to our leadership team where it was met with skepticism. We had previously repented with a service of reconciliation and hope. Why did we have to repent again? So many new people were now attending who were not involved in our past. How would they make sense of this?

We limited the scope of our repentance to our leadership team. While the framework we worked through certainly exposed some remaining sin, I still deeply regret being disobedient to God, even at the risk of alienating others. He had asked me to lead our congregation in repentance. I knew what He had asked, but I was willing to buy into the lie that repenting was on our terms.

John the Baptist preached "a baptism for the repentance for the forgiveness of sins" (Mark 1:4). Jesus' disciples baptized people as well (John 4:2). As an outward action that indicates a person's decision to repent and turn from their sin, baptism shows a commitment to follow Jesus.

Deciding to follow Jesus does not mean we will live a life without sin. In fact, we are unable to do so. Repentance is not a one-and-done situation. Jesus' call to Himself is a call to continuously allow the Holy Spirit to sift through our lives and lead us to repentance, each time causing us to grow more like Him.

A Time to Rejoice

The United States is one of the most affluent countries in the world. Some put it as number one, while others believe the relatively high number of billionaires in the U.S. skews the results. Even recognizing that millions of Americans are only one paycheck away from financial disaster, or that there are significant needs within our own communities, our lifestyles often reflect a measure of comfort that is well beyond what is lived elsewhere in the world.

At one point, our Missions and Outreach Team was looking for ways to walk alongside our local homeless population. They invited a leader of a local mission to one of their meetings to educate them on issues surrounding homelessness. What struck that team most was that although there were various causes, a significant percentage of that demographic was homeless due to mental health issues or addiction. Without addressing the root cause, homelessness will not go away.

When I worked part-time as a receptionist at an Episcopal Church south of Boston, homeless people stopped by frequently, knowing that the rector would provide a gas or food card or even take them out for a meal. At first, I wondered why they did not try to get back on their feet. In the naivety of youth, it did not make sense to me that someone would willingly choose to be homeless.

The more I dealt with the men and women who stopped by, the more I started to understand that this lifestyle was an active choice for many who had no intention or desire to change. Many did not want the responsibilities that were associated with becoming productive members of society.

This certainly does not apply to all persons or situations. It was only a general trend I noticed in those coming to this church for help, and it was eye-opening.

A TV series in 2017 entitled *Hunted* offered a $250,000 prize for a team of two who could elude capture by highly skilled investigators for twenty-eight days. What I found most fascinating is that seven of the nine captured teams were invariably tripped up by their reliance on the comfort of their everyday life. Captured teams included those who used an ATM and those who stayed with or received help from families or friends. It points to the difficulty of leaving our family and comfort behind!

God asked the Israelites to do just that every year following harvest. God had given instructions for celebrating a Feast of

Booths or Tabernacles (Sukkot) right after the Israelites were delivered from their bondage in Egypt "so that your generations may know that I had the sons of Israel live in booths when I brought them out from the land of Egypt. I am the Lord your God" (Lev 23:43). Each year, they were to erect temporary shelters (booths) and live in these shelters for the seven days of the feast.

While I greatly enjoy camping and look forward to planning trips, we often consult the weather forecast to try to outsmart mother nature and avoid the rain. I am not sure I would rejoice in a requirement to live in a booth for the same seven-day period every year.

Yet rejoicing is precisely how the Israelites responded when they heard this command. When Ezra read about this festival and the people realized it was the right time of the year to observe this festival, "there was great rejoicing" (Neh. 8:17). The people went to the hills and brought olive, myrtle, palm, and other leafy branches back to make the booths. They had repented and had every intention of living under God's Law moving forward.

This festival had not been held since the days of Joshua, son of Nun, approximately one thousand years earlier (Neh. 8:17). This festival would not even have been a tradition in the remotest memory of any family group. For all practical purposes, this was a new practice for the people, and they loved it. Embracing their heritage and the Law, they rejoiced in their God.

When a corporate change comes down from above, I must admit that it is sometimes not eagerly embraced. Multiple books have been written on effective change management, each with a slightly different approach. But the first steps are invariably the same: get early employee buy-in and support. The change is coming; the strategy is about how to get it accepted.

I once was a frontline observer as a new CEO began implementing changes across our organization. These changes greatly impacted the framework we worked under and were felt at all levels of the organization. Unfortunately, there was not a single decision that was in line with any recommendation from any book. It was off-the-scales awful, resulting in the loss of over half the employees within a few months, including many in senior leadership. The sad part is that no one disagreed with the new direction he was implementing, and the process was disastrous.

What can we learn from Nehemiah about implementing change? Look to the heart of your people. The Israelites were softened by worship and repentance. They longed to make things right with God and rejoiced when they heard of the opportunity to celebrate a festival.

If you plan to make changes in your life or where the change would impact others, do not ever let the change become more critical than understanding how it will affect others' hearts. If a change cannot be tied to worship or furthering people's knowledge and love of God, or if it is not accompanied by rejoicing, it may be time to rethink whether it is really something God is seeking to implement.

SUMMARY

God's Word is the bedrock of our faith. The foundation of spiritual leadership begins with an ever-deepening knowledge of His Word. This chapter explored three fundamental concepts requisite for your development as a leader. All of them stem from growing in your faith.

The first concept uncovered the importance of being

immersed in studying and learning God's Word. Continued development of our faith is critical to leading from within His will. As our understanding of God grows and we discover more about who He is, we will understand how far short we fall of His glory.

This leads to our second concept, where we become softened enough to allow Him to uncover our sin, leading to grief and repentance. We are not left there; He heals each area we are bold enough to turn over to Him, with the last concept being celebrating and rejoicing in the healing and restoration He brings.

These concepts are foundational to leading because others are watching. To the extent that they see your reliance upon Jesus, they will be willing to do the same. That is leadership—setting a course that others want to follow, and it is something to which God has called every one of us.

CONSIDER

Spiritual leadership starts with a personal commitment to grow and change as God leads. How do the concepts we explored in this chapter of deepening your knowledge of God's Word, grieving and repenting over your sin, and rejoicing in following Him help you lead others?

PRAYER

Holy Spirit, give me a thirst for Your Word that cannot be satisfied by programs, studies, or activities that simply keep me busy. Grant me opportunities to meet others and teach them about who You are. Continue to reveal areas of my heart that need You. May I model grief and repentance in my life. Most importantly, teach me to see others as You do, to feel Your compassion, and to genuinely love them as You love me, rejoicing in Your salvation. Amen.

∽9∾

Mighty Deeds

However, Thou art just in all that has come upon us; for Thou has dealt faithfully, but we have acted wickedly (Neh. 9:33).

IT IS NOT UNCOMMON TO SEE pebbles, stones, or small rocks on the graves of the deceased. This Jewish custom dates so far back in history that no documentation exists of when it began. This practice not only continues today but has started to be mimicked by other religions.

The meanings behind these rocks vary. Sometimes a stone is from a place of significance to the visitor or deceased. At other times, the actual stone is not as important as the remembrance associated with the stone's placement.

My daughter-in-law and I enjoy walking at a nearby park where a scenic 2.5-mile loop skirts the shores of Lake Washington. At the end of the park, there is a large boulder where walkers often leave small pillars of four to six stones taken from around its base. Every time I see this boulder with its stone pillars, I am reminded of biblical stones of remembrance.

The first mention of a stone of remembrance comes in Genesis 28:18, when Jacob spends the night sleeping on a stone pillow. He arose the following day, poured oil over the rock, and renamed the place Bethel, or house of God.

Here was where Jacob encountered God in a dream, and God promised Jacob that He chose him to continue the covenant God had made with Abraham and Isaac. Jacob consecrated the stone to honor and remember this event.

One of the most notable uses of stones occurs in Joshua 4:1-7 just after the Israelites had crossed through the Jordan River on dry land. God directed Joshua to have one man from each of the twelve tribes go into the middle of the riverbed and bring back one stone to the shore before the river returned.

They made a memorial out of these stones so when their descendants asked what the stone pile meant, they could remind them of the miraculous crossing of the Jordan River. Joshua 4:7 says, "So these stones shall become a memorial to the sons of Israel forever."

We must remember our past. Whether we use an actual stone or another item, a "stone of remembrance" is a catalyst for recalling a time when God interceded on our behalf. First Peter 2:5 reminds us that, "You also, as living stones, are being built up as a spiritual house for a holy priesthood." His actions, as they are embedded in our lives, become a living witness to what He has done for us.

The entire ninth chapter of Nehemiah acts as a stone of remembrance, exposing three more spiritual leadership concepts for us to explore. Each concept ties to a life of honor. First, we learn the importance of remembering God's work in the stories of our lives. The second concept keeps us centered and entirely devoted to Jesus. The final concept deals with our entitlement as God's children.

Your Story

My mother was one of six children. Throughout my youth, I loved hearing stories from her childhood. The stories were full of love, laughter, tragedy, and dreams. Her narratives came to life as she spoke of her parents, siblings, and grandmother.

I felt I was living in her stories as each story deepened my connection to my mother's family. Although I never met her parents, I think that I know them well. The power of a story connects us to others in a deep and lasting way.

People often view the Bible as a book of stories. While the Bible is more than just a collection of random accounts, I have realized that we more deeply connect to the One who participated in and authored them when we retell these same stories. Recounting and studying these stories allows them to come alive to us in a way that testifies to the Bible as God's living Word.

Beyond simply recording an event, each Bible story shows how God has worked in the lives of His people. Nearly 230 verses throughout the Bible exhort us to remember God's actions.

Trusting God is foundational to our faith. If we cannot trust God, how can we believe Him? Each time we remember how He has helped us in the past adds another piece to the foundation of trust. Over time, this leads to a solid base for our faith.

Nehemiah 9 begins with the Israelites spending half a day reading the Law, confessing their sins, and worshiping Yahweh. Following this time of learning, praise, and worship, the Levites recounted God's mighty deeds throughout the history of His people. This chapter provides fifty-three unique ways and times that God acted specifically for the benefit of the Israelites.

Each remembrance recalled a mighty deed God performed. A seemingly endless litany of involvement in the lives of His people brought to life the God of Abraham, Isaac, and Jacob for the people of Nehemiah. These stories strengthened their connection to God and became embedded in their souls as building blocks of faith.

I love to hear details of other people's lives. With each story, my amazement grows at how uniquely God draws each one of us to Himself. At one of the first memorial services I attended, there was a slide show and a beautiful write-up on the back of the program about that person's life. I remember thinking about how little I knew about that person and what an incredible individual he had been.

That impression of having missed out on knowing extraordinary things about people has grown with each memorial service I have attended. I have come to recognize that as I only share a small piece of someone's timeline, I will never fully know everything about that person. Even with close friends, I can still only know in part.

Contrast that with God. There has never been a time when God has not known you thoroughly and completely, regardless of whether you followed Him. Psalm 139:13, 16 states, "For Thou didst form my inward parts; Thou didst weave me in my mother's womb. Thine eyes have seen my unformed substance; and in Thy book they were all written, the days that were ordained for me, when as yet there was not one of them."

Beyond anyone on earth, God knows every part of your story from before you were born. Knowing you intimately, He also knows the best way to reach your heart with His love and wants to be part of your story. No one else can ever say that.

One of our responsibilities when I once served on our nominating committee was to "identify and encourage lay participation in church ministries and programs." Our committee decided to focus on the "identify" portion of this task. In discussing how much we enjoyed and learned from reading about people's lives and giftings at their memorial services, we decided not to wait until it was too late!

We ran a series of monthly bulletin inserts that interviewed random people at church. It was a chance to have our congregation get to know someone's story— without waiting for their memorial. It was amazing to see and hear of the conversations these people had with others they had not spoken to frequently, all due to these personal highlights.

Recognize how God is moving in your life's story. Remembering and telling others what God has done creates a solid foundation of faith. He has acted in the past; He will act again. You do not need to go through a time of crisis to see or recognize God's actions. He is faithful to work in both good and bad times. Psalm 106:2 states, "Who can speak of the mighty deeds of the Lord, or can show forth all His praise?" Let us be the ones who do so; let it begin with us.

Boomerangs and Yo-yos

I recently learned the difference between "boomerang" and "yo-yo" relationships. In simplest terms, a boomerang relationship occurs when someone breaks off a relationship to start dating someone new, realizes that the original relationship was better than what they now have, breaks up with the new person, and goes back to the first person. The boomerang effect is typified by there never being a complete emotional break between the parties.

In contrast, the dysfunction of a yo-yo relationship is internal to the relationship itself. Neither party is seeking to leave, but either person's emotional availability switches on and off. Typically, one party expresses warmth and openness, pulls back emotionally, then resumes the warmth and openness.

Both types of relationships are unhealthy and emotionally exhausting. One major difficulty is that a person engaged in one of these relationships usually cannot recognize the inherent dysfunction in the situation. Only when the individual looks backward after the relationship has ended do these unhealthy patterns become visible.

Decisions involving relationships are frequently driven by emotion, whereas cognitive reasoning is often a better choice for selecting a course of action from among several alternatives. Good leaders tend to rely on cognitive reasoning by ignoring their emotional responses and weighing the facts before deciding what they believe will be the most effective course of action. Indecisive people are often paralyzed by the belief that only one right choice exists, yet they are not sure which one it is.

Watching a decisive person try to help an indecisive person make a choice can be painful. Picking new flatware, dishes, or carpet will often reveal where someone falls on the decisive scale. Both types of people go through a completely different decision-making processes. Ultimately, they will decide, even if the indecisive person's conclusion is a default due to their inability to choose.

———

Throughout the Old Testament, numerous leaders are identified within Israel and the nearby nations. These (typically male) leaders are often presented as decisive or impassioned individuals in literature and paintings. An image that comes to mind is Rembrandt's painting of Moses coming down from Mount Sinai with the Ten Commandments held aloft, clouds and storms swirling around him.

Contrast that to the relationship between the Israelites and God, which seems to fluctuate between being like a boomerang and a yo-yo. When in boomerang mode, the people are seduced by other cultures and gods and try them out for a time before returning. Other times, the relationship is more of a yo-yo, with the people turning away from and then back to God in a regular, repetitious pattern.

Regardless of the strength or decisiveness of the leader, the Israelites tend to be indecisive followers. Time and again, they stray from following Yahweh. No sooner has God performed a mighty deed than they seem to turn their backs on Him. They cannot seem to make up their mind to follow God wholeheartedly, for all time. Observing the dysfunctional patterns is pretty easy hundreds of years later, but they were not evident at the time.

As the Levites recounted story after story of God's mighty and faithful acts in Nehemiah 9, it is apparent that these stories intertwined with the times when the people turned away from God. Included are phrases such as "became stubborn and would not listen" (Neh. 9:16), "became disobedient and rebelled" (Neh. 9:26), "as soon as they had rest, they did evil again" (Neh. 9:28), and "they acted arrogantly and did not listen" (Neh. 9:29). They did not remember what God had done, they killed the prophets God sent, and they sinned.

Throughout the recitation, God is unchanging. He is always there, always constant, and always ready to take them back.

Nehemiah 9:17 says, "But Thou art a God of forgiveness, gracious and compassionate, slow to anger and abounding in lovingkindness." Nehemiah 9:31 says, "Nevertheless, in Thy great compassion Thou didst not make an end of them or forsake them, for Thou art a gracious and compassionate God." Over and over, He pulls His people back to Himself. He made a covenant with Abraham that survives even their unfaithfulness.

We must guard against moving off-center from wholehearted commitment to Jesus. Off-center can be when we rely on rote prayers or a quick reading through our daily devotion rather than spending time with Jesus. We may join activities or groups that are more social than seeking to follow God's direction. Our churches can be off-center when they become social clubs, when cliques make it difficult for newcomers to feel a place of connection, or when large donors manipulate decisions.

These scenarios can pull us from a single-minded focus on following Jesus and Him only. If you are involved in any groups, you have influence. Being a spiritual leader means using that influence to pull the group back into alignment with Jesus.

As early as Genesis 6:5, the Scripture says, "Then the Lord saw that the wickedness of man was great on the earth, and that every intent of the thoughts of his heart was only evil continually." That says it all. As hard as we try, we will never be able to maintain constancy in our following of Jesus; we will fail.

We need to remember that God does not change. His constancy is always waiting for us to return to Him. We must occasionally take a critical look at ourselves and our ministries to course-correct, if needed, to stay in the center of His will.

Bargain or Entitlement

In court, most criminal cases end in plea bargains; very few make it to trial. Reasons vary, but deals are typically negotiated well before pretrial hearings. It can seem in everyone's best interest to dispatch a case by agreeing to a compromise. No one is fully satisfied, but the involved parties agree on what is considered a reasonable middle ground.

Negotiating and bargaining are part of the American lifestyle. We clip coupons and look for sales. From negotiating the price of a new car or house to shopping on BOGO (buy one/get one) days, we are constantly looking for bargains.

JCPenney eliminated all sales several years ago by offering "everyday value" pricing. No sales, just low prices. It failed abysmally. People did not want low prices; they wanted to feel like they were snagging a deal. Psychologically, people want to be on the receiving end of a bargain, which explains the mania that occurs on Black Friday (the day after Thanksgiving) or the day after Christmas.

When I was a little girl, my mother would get my sister and me up early the day after Christmas to go shopping; all Christmas decorations were sold at half price that day. We would scope out the Christmas section of our favorite department store a day or two in advance to know what we would grab.

The hysteria was incredible. Large mobs of (mainly) women would stand for hours outside the store, wanting to get the best spot for when the doors opened. Panic ensued if another door opened before yours, and you saw people streaming into the store.

I recall seeing women running up the "down" escalators to beat the crowds or cramming carts full of everything within arms' reach, only to sort through and decide to keep or discard items while waiting in line. Lines for the checkout could easily take over an hour.

I have a cherished set of four porcelain angels from one of the mad after-Christmas sales when I was in 7th grade. The six-foot-tall plastic Christmas tree of my youth came from yet another after-Christmas sale. It was pandemonium, yet fun in a strange way. We had to be early, pick the right door, and shop for all we were worth. The bargain was worth it.

There is a subtle difference between a good bargain and negotiating. It is a matter of entitlement. As Nehemiah 9 closes, there is recognition that the Israelites are coming out of a boomerang season in Babylon.

Although still identifying as Israelites, they recognized that they had fallen away from knowing and living within God's Law. In Nehemiah 9:34–37, they acknowledged their sin, confessing that they did not serve God or turn from their evil deeds. The chapter ends with, "Now because of all this we are making an agreement in writing; and on the sealed document are the names of our leaders, our Levites and our priests" (Neh. 9:38).

Within their confession, the Israelites embedded a complaint: they were now slaves on the land God had once given them. Based on the stories we just read in Nehemiah 9, His judgment against them, including this consequence, appears justified.

By what authority do they now come into His presence and question His actions? They were not trying to bargain with God. They believed they were entitled to relief based on their covenant relationship with Him.

Children will always try to negotiate a reduction in punishment. They will enter a plea bargain (or beg) to minimize a consequence. My husband often annoyingly says, "You can do whatever you want, as long as you are willing to pay the consequence."

Psalm 82:6 states, "And all of you are sons of the Most High." Our status as His children is confirmed by Galatians 3:26–27: "For you are all sons of God through faith in Christ Jesus. For all of you who were baptized into Christ have clothed yourselves with Christ."

The fact that we are in a relationship with God means that we are entitled to come to Him with everything. As His children, He welcomes us to bring all our concerns to Him. We are not just bargaining and hoping for a good deal; we have the right of entitlement to come and plead our case.

When I was in high school, my father rightly disciplined me for something I had done. In the heat of the moment, I screamed, "I hate you!" and stormed to my room. Many years later, I recalled this event to him and asked for his forgiveness. He smiled and told me he had forgiven me before I had even left the room that day.

In His role as our Father, we must also expect and be willing to accept God's discipline. "It is for discipline that you endure; God deals with you as with sons; for what son is there whom his father does not discipline?" (Heb. 12:7). Discipline does not take away our right of entitlement to come before Him. While we know that God disciplines us because He loves us, He does not mind when we plead with Him for leniency. We must be careful not to get stuck in unforgiveness due to our deserved discipline.

The mark of a leader is to model the behavior of the

Israelites for others to see and follow. Never be afraid to beg God for leniency or forgiveness. Come to God as His child and claim the blood of Jesus as your entitlement. Bargain, negotiate, and plead with Him. While He still has the final say, you know He will always respond as a loving Father.

SUMMARY

This chapter explores several spiritual leadership principles that revolve around the mighty deeds of God. The result of God acting in your life should be a cause for celebration, yet that is not always the case. The concepts in this chapter will allow you to be an example, a leader, for others to follow in response to what God is doing in their lives.

First, we covered the importance of looking back and remembering how God has moved and worked in our lives. Stones of remembrance are one technique to keep these stories alive.

Our second concept covered differing responses to God's mighty deeds. Many of us turn away from God even after He has acted mightily on our behalf. We boomerang away, looking for greener grass, only to return as we again realize nothing else can replace Him in our life. Keeping your focus and devotion on Him is vital.

The third leadership component deals with understanding your entitlement to come before Him with everything you are experiencing. You do not need to bargain with Him. Rather, claiming your right as His child, you can enter His presence boldly. God welcomes you to come to Him, always.

CONSIDER

Not all histories are beautiful; some are painful. Regardless of your past, God's mighty deeds can be evident in your life. Where does God show up in your story? Do those stories cause you to cling more tightly to Him? As His child, claim your right to come before Him in everything.

PRAYER

O God, I come to you today with a humble and contrite spirit. Show me anew the mighty deeds You have done in my life. Help me to sing praises and share these deeds with others. I confess that I often turn away from You even after You have done amazing things. Forgive me. May I accept Your discipline and embrace what You are teaching me. I fully submit to Your authority, asking and pleading as Your child for Your grace to be equal to Your discipline. Amen.

～10～

Future Focused

Now the rest of the people . . . are taking on themselves a curse and an oath to walk in God's law" (Neh. 10:28–29).

In 1804, President Thomas Jefferson commissioned Meriwether Lewis to explore the lands west of the Mississippi River in the hope of charting a transcontinental water route between the East and West Coasts that might support commercial traffic. Along with his friend, William Clark, this two-year, eight-thousand-mile expedition provided a wealth of new geographic, ecological, and social information about this previously uncharted territory. During the journey, Lewis and Clark encountered treacherous terrain, harsh weather, injuries, starvation, disease, and attacks by hostile Native Americans.

A then-popular scientific notion believed that nature was, in essence, symmetrical, leading the expedition to anticipate that the topography they traversed on the east side of the Continental Divide would match what they would encounter to the west. Instead, upon cresting the Continental Divide, they found wave upon wave of mountain peaks for as far as they could see. Gently drifting downriver to the Pacific Ocean was not going to happen. They threw all their plans away; they had to innovate to survive.

The expedition's success is attributed to two overriding factors: meticulous preparation and staying the course. To prepare, Lewis studied medicine, botany, natural history, astronomy, zoology, geology, and map-making. Regardless of obstacles, he set an end goal and stayed true to that course.

For vacation, my husband and I enjoy car camping throughout the United States. While there is little to no territory left that would echo the type of trek undertaken by Lewis and Clark, the incredible geographic and topographic changes we encounter as we drive across the country continue to captivate and pull us back for more.

We carefully plan our trips with the miles we drive each day and, more importantly, where we plan to stop each night, with critical components being to time our arrival before dark and ensure our campsite has a clean drinking water supply. Preparation is vital, especially if we fly somewhere to begin our camping expedition. We check that we have the right gear for the time of year and terrain we will traverse.

In Nehemiah 10, the Israelites come together to chart a course for their future. They built the wall, exhibited unity, and learned and embraced the law of Moses, acknowledging their place in the story of their people. Now, they proactively set a course to prevent backsliding. This chapter is less of an aspirational, idealistic vision of their future than the specific details on how they will follow God. They chart a course to reach their goal.

This chapter takes us back to our last few concepts in situational leadership, focusing on a life of freedom. We will first explore the idea of oaths regarding binding ourselves to Jesus. Secondly, we will remember that in all things, He is to receive the first fruits of our labor. Lastly, we will look at the attitude of our hearts when we serve. Being a leader requires us to learn to be Jesus' servant.

An Oath

How many times have you ever made a promise? Most likely, the number is too vast to count. What about a vow? Considering this may cause a few of us to pause. This number may be a much smaller, specific number, the most common type being a wedding vow. When we get to oaths, an even smaller number would have taken an oath, such as being sworn into office.

These three verbally binding commitments tend to escalate in order of significance or implication of their impact as we move from a promise to a vow to an oath. A promise is when one gives their word to another to do (or not do) something. A vow is defined as a solemn promise to perform some act or behave in a specified manner, while an oath is a sacred pledge that attests to the truth of a statement or binds one's future actions not dissimilar to a legal contract.

I have made few vows in my lifetime; however, about a year before his death, I made a vow to our lead pastor that for as long as our bylaws allowed, I would not speak of stepping aside as the church chair. This vow was necessary. When I assumed the position, I considered the role of chair only loosely binding.

While committed to my vow, I was willing to step aside if the previous lead pastor or others believed God was asking me to do so. When things got difficult, I began questioning my calling as church chair, which frustrated our current lead pastor. The long and short of it was that I made a vow and intended to live up to my commitment.

About a week after our pastor's death, my husband and I went away for a few days to a small lakeside cabin with no cellphone reception or internet. It was much-needed time away, a chance to reset our life and ministry following the death of this dearly beloved man. During this time, I heard God clearly and gently say, "You are released."

These words were difficult to hear and accept. I completed six years in leadership and was eligible to serve one more three-year term. I still felt that I had much to do. I also genuinely loved being chair. Yet, God had given me the release command. It was time for someone new; the Lord had released me from my vow, and I needed to obey.

Nehemiah 9 concludes with the Israelites creating a sealed agreement that charted the course for their future. Nehemiah 10 delineates requirements that would enable them to keep God's Law, commandments, ordinances, and statutes. This binding document's intent was to ensure the people remained faithful to God.

This agreement specifically named Nehemiah and eighty-two leaders, priests, and Levites. Following these named individuals, the chapter includes a list of an entire litany of people who also were committed to following this agreement: gate-keepers, singers, temple servants, wives, sons, and daughters. This list included all who chose to separate themselves from the people of the land and those old enough to understand (Neh. 10:28).

At this point, a surprising thing occurred. Beyond simply making an oath before God, they then unanimously agreed to add a curse to that oath (Neh. 10:29) should they fail in any aspect of meeting it. This oath was not easy in the first place, so tying failure to specific consequences indicated the magnitude and seriousness of how they viewed it.

Having just studied the Law, the knowledge of what they were taking on was evident, particularly the strict admonitions surrounding vows and oaths in Numbers 30, entitled "Laws of Vows." Numbers 30:2 states, "If a man makes a vow to the Lord, or takes an oath to bind himself with a binding obligation, he shall not violate his work; he shall do according to all that proceeds out of his mouth." Deuteronomy 23:21 says, "When you make a vow to the Lord your God, you shall not delay to pay it, for it would be sin in you, and the Lord your God will surely require it of you."

For oaths today, we can go beyond the warnings in the Old Testament. James 5:12 includes the admonition that we should not swear, "either by heaven or by earth or with any other oath; but let your yes be yes, and your no, no; so that you may not fall under judgment." This verse mimics similar words from Jesus in Matthew 5:33–37. These verses lead us to question an oath's place as we guide those around us.

We do not need to make an oath to follow a specific course of action when our lives are already bound to Jesus. Jesus offers a simple and compelling invitation to "Follow Me." As we accept that invitation, the Holy Spirit begins to live in us, and our lives will start to look more and more like Jesus.

We should expect course corrections and realignment throughout our ministry. But, as we live in the power of the Holy Spirit, our yes or no will suffice; those we lead will trust our word. If Jesus leads us as we lead our churches, we will want to continue along that path. No other oath is needed.

First Fruits

Financial gifts have a tremendous impact on our ability to minister and serve the communities around us. Statistics show that Christians give approximately 2.5 percent of their income to their church. Other statistics indicate that 3-5 percent of Americans tithe (defined as giving 10 percent of income).

In the American church, although giving is down, pastors tend to focus a sermon only rarely on biblical tithing. Not wanting to come across as greedy or focused only on money, tithing has become a taboo subject in many congregations.

Growing up in the Episcopal Church, I witnessed a yearly "canvassing" effort each fall. Several men would come to our house to meet with us or pick up my parents' pledge card, which contained their financial commitment for the upcoming year. Based on these pledges, our church developed next year's ministries and programs. This rhythm became natural in our church life.

At my current church, this is not the norm. Congregants do not make pledges. Instead, my church makes ministry plans based on anticipated giving for the upcoming year. Being a nonprofit organization, the budget presented to the congregation for approval always needed to be net zero. Some years see more giving than anticipated, and some require us to take from our reserves to cover the gap.

———

Many are surprised to learn that Jesus discussed money more often than heaven or hell or faith and prayer combined. Nearly 30 percent of His parables specifically refer to money or the use of money to teach a spiritual truth. Why was the subject of money such a topic of interest? Far from being obsessed with money, Jesus knew that how we live with and relate to our money is an issue of the heart.

The Bible mentions tithing as early as Genesis, where Abram gives a tenth of all he has to Melchizedek (Gen. 14:17–

20). Leviticus 27:30–33 and Numbers 18:21–28 established the Law for tithing, indicating the people should give a tenth of all produce, flocks, and cattle to support the priest's work. Deuteronomy 26:12–13 says foreigners, orphans, and widows should be included as recipients of tithe distribution. Tithing was not an afterthought. Instead, the Israelites were to give it out of the first of the produce and flocks.

Nehemiah established expectations for giving patterns as he continued setting the course for his people in Nehemiah 10. The oath included a commitment for the Israelites to give a tithe from the ground's and trees' first fruits, the firstborn of the sons and cattle and the herds and flocks, and the first of the dough, wine, and oil. The first of everything was a critical component of tithing as they set their course: they would give to God first.

Giving these first fruits was not an ideal the people sought. It was a commitment. Remember that the leaders and people had bound themselves to this agreement and even swore an oath to abide by it. These were not just words on a piece of paper but a promise made with the complete foreknowledge and agreement of the people.

As you build a ministry focused more on Jesus than programs and activities, God will draw people to Himself. Giving our first fruits should not be a burden; it should be a natural outpouring of gratitude for what God has done in our lives.

Nowhere does the Bible talk about the numbers or size of a congregation. Rather, we are encouraged to "seek first His kingdom and His righteousness" (Matthew 6:33). We can expand this beyond personal application to the way we lead.

If people are to give generously from their first fruits, we should do all we can to ensure that the course of any ministry is first set on following Jesus. Those in ministry should never be afraid to ask people to support their ministries; money should never be a taboo subject. If Jesus talked about it, we should as well. Our responsibility is to ensure that any discussion on money does not apply pressure or guilt to give more.

I am sure we have each encountered people who get hung up on the exact definition of the 10 percent tithe. Does it apply to before- or after-tax income? Does giving money to non-Christian nonprofits count? I suggest that if people ask those types of questions, they miss the point. It is a matter of the heart.

As we allow our people to be involved in and shape the course of our ministry, giving will follow. By teaching biblical principles of giving, we can then stand back and allow the Holy Spirit to lead people to give as He leads.

Even if you are not involved in a ministry where others are directly supporting you financially, this section still applies to how you are to lead. As a leader, you are to model a sound approach to giving. The recipient of all first fruits is God, and He knows the condition of your heart when you give.

As your life aligns with this command, you can mentor and train those around you to give sacrificially. Nothing is easy about giving first fruits. Setting those first fruits aside for Jesus puts the rest of our earnings in the proper perspective. Model what you want others to follow.

Service

Think of a time you went to dinner or attended an event where the service was superb. Contrast that with another time when the service was not quite up to par. What made the difference? I travel extensively for work and attend many dinners and events. My expectations for good service include frequent but not invasive check-ins, refilling my water without asking or intruding on conversation, and timely food delivery with leisurely eating.

A server comes alongside and is present, but not part of, the meal or event. That individual is there to be attentive to my needs but remains in the background unless called upon. Thinking through my expectations, I realize that food service is truly an art!

Servers are not typically paid well, and many rely on tips to make ends meet. On some occasions, we have not left a good tip. I am sure that a poor tip did not lead our server to perform better for the next customer. These days I commonly double-check my bill as some restaurants now add a set gratuity. Before I became accustomed to checking, some lucky waitstaff received up to 35 percent or more for a tip.

My parents were not the best tippers. Sometimes when they took us out for dinner, we would ask to leave a tip. I would often provide a tip to the waiter mid-meal or go back to the table before leaving the restaurant to add a bit more to the tip my parents had left. We did not do this out of disrespect for my parents but to provide a reasonable gratuity for today's standards.

A significant difference lies between a server and a servant. While both may perform similar services, the distinction is unmistakable. A server willingly meets our needs; a servant is under an obligation to do so. A servant is one whose person and liberty are under the authority of a master. Both receive compensation. The difference is a matter of the heart.

Nehemiah continued to set the course for the Israelites by ensuring that caring for the house of God was part of the plan.

He wanted to be sure that he considered its future needs. The Levites, priests, gatekeepers, and singers were included in the receipt of offerings and tithes, substantiating the importance the people had placed on the continued support of service to God. These positions were full-time, and these men gave up any other possible livelihood to serve God.

Chapter 10 closes with Nehemiah firmly charging the people not to neglect the house of the Lord (v. 39). Beyond the tithes and offerings mentioned, the expectation was clear that this service to God should be something that came from the heart. These men were not servants, nor was it just a job to be carried out; they were to willingly devote themselves to serving God.

Most of us can identify several people who have the gift of serving (Rom. 12:7). These people typically like to be behind the scenes in cooking, cleaning, serving meals, or washing dishes. They often prefer not to be pointed out. Being able to expend their gift in the service of others is enough recognition. I think of one woman whose heart is so attuned to serving that suspending activities due to COVID-19 has been extremely difficult for her.

One translation of the word deacon (*diakonos*) is "servant." Depending on the denomination, deacons are often assigned to care for the physical needs of the people. The need for congregational care shows up in the early church in Acts 6:1–6 where seven men are selected to serve as deacons, allowing the apostles to focus on prayer and the word.

During this pandemic, our deacons have been the lifeline to many who are shuttered at home. These gifted individuals have held our congregation together more than any other ministry team. While not meeting together physically, I have found that we are more connected to each other through this specific ministry of service.

While it is easy to relegate this task to those specially gifted, Acts 16:17 reminds us that we are "bond-servants of the Most High God." As a Christian, I am a bond-servant of Jesus. I am to serve Him willingly and with all my heart in all things. Paul encourages us to seek the same mindset as Jesus in our relationships with others, specifically noting that we are to take "the very nature of a servant" (Phil. 2:7).

Not recognizing the importance of servanthood in leading well can be tempting. Leaders are often the go-to people who know everything. If they do not perceive an answer, good leaders will usually figure one out (or make one up). They tend to have proactive, resilient, motivated, flexible, courageous, and enthusiastic personalities.

In searching through several secular resources on the characteristics of a leader, not one of my resources mentioned servanthood. This omission is a critical distinction between leadership in the world and the church. While the term servant leadership is common, leaders can become so busy with their church's day-to-day running and success that they begin to lose sight of the importance of this concept.

Leading any task or activity should, first and foremost, begin with ensuring you have the mindset of Jesus. Humility and obedience to Him should be at the forefront of all forms of leadership. At no time should the question arise of who the leader is: it is not you. Serving Jesus first and foremost will allow you to prioritize and approach your leadership and ministries with the mindset of Jesus and let God have His rightful place.

SUMMARY

This chapter covered leadership concepts for looking at where God has or may be calling you. Understanding that leadership starts with having the mindset of Jesus is critical. Everything else, including setting the course of ministry or life, should spring from that. He wants you to lead through any situation you may encounter, focusing on Him. Remember, you may have been placed in a specific situation to allow you to lead others into learning what it means to have a Jesus-focused mindset.

The first concept explored the application of oaths. Used extensively throughout the Old Testament, Jesus sets us free from rigid adherence to oath-taking. To the extent you are bound to Jesus when you become a Christian, you are bound to keep your word. Other oaths are unnecessary.

Secondly, we looked at the concept of being unafraid of discussing the things Jesus talked about, including finances. As a leader, you must model what it means to give God your first fruits in everything you have.

Finally, your leadership should approach any ministry to which God has called you from a perspective of service. Growing as a servant-leader begins with humility and obedience. What flows from your heart reflects who Jesus is to you.

CONSIDER

Thinking about where God may lead you in the future can be overwhelming. How do the leadership concepts of being bound to God, giving Him your first fruits, and serving with a heart of humility and obedience provide a solid footing from which to start?

PRAYER

Lord God, may my yes be yes, and my no be no. Please give me the courage to follow through on my word. Teach me the humility and obedience needed to become a servant leader so that I may be bold enough to challenge Your people to give to You out of the first fruits of their lives. Each time I hear the words "Follow Me," may they awaken a renewed desire to follow wherever You lead and push aside all the desires and plans I have created on my own. Amen.

∾11∾

Understand Others

Now the leaders of the people lived in Jerusalem, but the rest of the people cast lots to bring one out of ten to live in Jerusalem, the holy city, while nine-tenths remained in the other cities" (Neh. 11:1).

THE PREMISE OF THE MOVIE *Field of Dreams* is that "if you build it, he will come." It is a movie of hope, second chances, and reconciliation, all centered around the love of baseball. The main character, Ray Kinsella, hears a voice telling him to build a baseball diamond in his cornfield in Iowa.

Ray did not have any idea what the outcome would be or even who "he" was. Willing to take a chance, and acting on his dream against all logical reasoning, he stepped out in faith, completely unsure where it would lead.

This movie provides an apt description of what many of us hope for in our lives—second chances and reconciliation. As a community of believers, we are also part of a family that is sometimes mired in turmoil but still committed to each other, bound by our love for Jesus. The basis for many callings and ministries is what we believe we have heard God say. We act, anticipating God's abundant supply.

Nehemiah 11 through Nehemiah 12:26 documents the creation of a coordinated system of procedures to ensure lasting protection of the wall. A few months had transpired since the people completed the wall. In fact, the dedication of the wall had not yet occurred (spoiler alert for chapter 12). It was time for Nehemiah to implement the final logistics needed to maintain the Israelites' ongoing safety.

Within this section of Nehemiah, we see three unique types of people that you may encounter as you lead, develop, and then protect your ministry. Nehemiah shows us how to blend these people into the body of Christ without neglecting our first and foremost call to follow Jesus. Working with all types of people is a core leadership skill and ties directly to a life of service. Stepping out in faith to do what God has called you to do includes working with everyone He provides, regardless of personality.

Our first concept will explore those who are known as super-volunteers. These people are at every event and are the first to volunteer for anything. Understanding how to integrate them into your network without them taking over or superseding others is a crucial step to a healthy ministry.

Secondly, many groups include those who consider themselves the elite or who's who, entitled to special benefits or voice. Various reasons cause this attitude, such as length of time in service, money, or their relationship with you. We will explore concepts to limit their ability to negatively impact where God is leading.

Finally, we encounter the surprise category of unlikely supporters, those we might never imagine would be early adopters and influencers. Leadership concepts for this section focus on identifying and helping them engage their gifts.

Any Volunteers?

Many years ago, we entered our daughter in a drawing to attend a choice lottery school for her middle and high school years. Any child within the school district was eligible to apply; however, the acceptance pool was small due to the sheer number of applications. The benefits of attending included a smaller student-to-teacher ratio, block classes, senior projects, and a critical focus on preparation for AP courses. The strict expectations placed on the students were matched with solid academic support. The school intended the drawing to keep the attendance numbers low while providing every child in the district the same likelihood of getting in.

Considered one of the top schools in the district, ranked second in Washington State, and seventy-fifth in national rankings with a score of 99.58/100 (2020), the prestige of attending cannot be overstated. The thrill of seeing our daughter's name on the list was unforgettable.

Nehemiah 11 opens with a lottery underway to move people from the surrounding countryside into the new walled city of Jerusalem. The city did not have a critical sustaining mass, and without enough people living in the city, the wall was vulnerable to attack and renewed destruction. In a spirit of national patriotism, volunteers entered their names in a drawing for the chance to move to the city.

Many of these people had lived in the countryside for years. They were well-established and would have had land, property, and livestock. Country life was safe, and they lived in relative comfort. Volunteering for the lottery meant these men and their families would sacrifice their safety and comfort to protect Jerusalem and the new wall.

One out of every ten males was selected to relocate, and Nehemiah 11:2 says, "The people blessed all the men who volunteered to live in Jerusalem." These families willingly gave up their way of life, all that was familiar, to populate a major city.

Jesus said, "Everyone who has left houses or brothers or sisters or father or mother or children or farms for My name's sake, shall receive many times as much, and shall inherit eternal life" (Matt. 19:29). Jesus still calls us to leave everything associated with our past life to follow Him.

We may not be required to leave our homes or livelihoods physically, but it certainly requires giving up anything more important than our devotion to Him. Sometimes this requires us to take a hard look at where we spend our time.

Most groups are familiar with those who are super-volunteers. These people are the first to sign up . . . for anything. They work tirelessly on behalf of whatever they have signed up for, are often satisfied with remaining behind the scenes, and prefer no accolades. I would venture to say that no group or ministry can be without these people.

You must be aware of the potential danger of these volunteers transitioning—sometimes without their noticing—from being solely motivated by a desire to serve Jesus to doing so for other reasons. Now they may volunteer because no one else is willing, or because they can do it better than anyone else, or even because they have always done it.

Volunteers who started out wanting to use their gifts for Jesus can become stuck in a place where their hearts have shifted, and their motivation has become skewed toward self-glory. One of the easiest ways to identify this is when someone leads a ministry for years without ever intending to let someone else take over.

Succession planning is a big topic in the corporate world. As baby boomers start to near retirement, interest increases in guaranteeing the continuing success of a firm as people begin to leave. One company I know had every leader develop a formal succession plan so the individuals identified to take over would be ready. Companies understand that a lack of succession planning can quickly wipe out any gains they have made with untested or less knowledgeable replacements.

We should "bake" succession planning into our ministries. Leaders should discuss with anyone volunteering for a new position, particularly those who may be in the category of super-volunteers, how they will identify and train someone to replace them. This process also needs to include those volunteering for leadership.

I frequently hear when someone new steps into a role previously occupied by someone else that they had been hoping for years to have the opportunity to serve in that position. How unfortunate that sometimes potential volunteers can't share a gift or calling because someone else is unwilling to step aside and let a new person lead "their" ministry.

Scripture exhorts us: "Do nothing from selfishness or empty conceit, but with humility of mind let each of you regard one another as more important than himself; do not merely look out for your own personal interests, but also for the interests of others" (Phil 2:3–4). This directive describes having the mind of Christ. By arming ourselves and our volunteers with this mindset, we remain in a place of serving Jesus from the heart.

Who's Who

When I was in college, *Who's Who* invited me to join their community. For a small fee, membership in this exclusive group means they will include your name and biographical information in an annual publication along with other prominent and influential people. The oldest and best-known publication of *Who's Who* in Britain has been around since 1849, with over thirty-four thousand individuals, including such notable persons as Sir Isaac Newton, Charles Darwin, and Stephen Hawking.

I declined the invitation. To my knowledge, I had not yet done anything noteworthy other than receiving a few scholarships. My potential was still untapped; I was just beginning to be poised to start my life. It felt disingenuous to consider joining a group just so I could have my name published in a book, mainly since I highly doubted anyone in the book ever looked to see the other people included.

I was reminded of when I was young, and the telephone White Pages were delivered to our door. We would immediately open it and find our name, address, and telephone number. We were someone! It felt much along those lines. I did not need to be listed in a book to know that Jesus already considered me a person of value.

After selecting family groups to move to Jerusalem, Nehemiah then listed the priests, Levites, temple servants, and gatekeepers chosen for service to God. These were the Who's Who of the Israelites, who had the most significant responsibility in Israel—serving Yahweh in His temple.

A definite status was associated with being a priest or Levite. People would honor and defer to them on most matters of the Law. They had tremendous power and were often teachers and judges. Even today, they are considered the "religious elite" of the Jewish faith.

Jesus had a way of cutting through to the heart of the matter. Over time, some priests, Levites, and Pharisees had begun to see themselves as more important than others. They expected people to defer to them in public and invite them to the highest seats of honor at banquets.

Jesus did not mince words when speaking of those who expected favor based on their religious practices. He likened Pharisees to "white-washed tombs" (Matt. 23:27) who were beautiful on the outside but dead on the inside. They maintained a system that was more about outward appearance than inward faith.

―――――

Money, longevity in a ministry, or even a relationship with you as a leader can bring expectations of entitlement or having a more significant say in discussions and decisions. The expectations brought on by a sense of entitlement can be difficult to counter. Unfortunately, it is easy to find examples of this type of behavior. Leaders must address it immediately and overtly.

Volunteer labor was instrumental in building our church. Several people contributed vast sums of money and time over several building phases to create our current facility. It was built in love, with labor and money given freely. Regrettably, over time, the attitude of some of these volunteers began to trend toward ownership.

I recall one incident when I led our women ministries team. In the main hall, two built-in cabinets contained a series of pull-out drawers. The drawers at one time housed table-cloths and other linens. Many years previous, they had been handcrafted by one of the volunteer church builders, a man who loved woodworking and carpentry. The work was exquisite, but the location no longer served its purpose.

The women ministries team wanted to remove these cabinets and update the niches to allow for displays that might be more attractive and welcoming to newcomers. Our pastor told us that the cabinets were not to be removed as he did not want to risk losing this couple's donations. This decision was based solely on the positional authority he gave this couple rather than what might have been in the church's best interest.

We are exhorted in James 4:10: "Humble yourselves in the presence of the Lord, and He will exalt you." Those who see themselves as the "who's who" in our churches are a force to be reckoned with. The key is to not concede to their perceived power nor cave to their demands. We cannot make others humble, but knowing God has called us to humility can be helpful.

Humility is not being powerless in the face of pride. It is a calling to act from a position of complete dependence upon God. When we decide to work by where God is leading—regardless of demands or expectations by others—we strip them of their power. Going in this direction is not easy when finances could be impacted, but we are not exhibiting leadership for a ministry to be held hostage to accommodate someone's personal whims.

Be willing to stand your ground, even in the face of those pushing for decisions based on a perceived entitlement. Lean on Jesus to supply your needs, even if it means reframing your ministry.

Unlikely Support

In the early to mid-eighties, many companies in corporate America were required to meet hiring quotas for women and minorities. At the time of my graduation, only about one in ten engineers were women, with even fewer women engineers in corporate leadership roles.

Although I knew I was hired in my first entry-level position because of my gender, I told myself that I would not care. Regardless of the reasons behind my hiring, I would prove that I could do the job.

It would be nice to say that race, gender, sexuality, or nationality should not come into play during hiring. Everyone should be treated equally without regard to these factors. Unfortunately, that is not the case. Most companies now include Equal Employment Opportunity (EEO) statements in their employee handbooks and vow that everyone will have the same opportunity to succeed regardless of these factors.

While breaking through geo-political and socio-economic barriers is part of how we do business today, this was not the case for Nehemiah. No inclusion plans were available for marginalized people. Strict boundaries existed between classes, races, and gender. People in one arena would not necessarily cross over to support others in a different sphere. Therefore, it is a bit of a surprise to learn there was a secret supporter of reestablishing the Israelite community in Jerusalem—King Artaxerxes.

It was not surprising that the king supported rebuilding the wall around Jerusalem. Providing financial support and supplies to ensure its success extended his control and power in the region and established a strong outpost. The surprise is that King Artaxerxes did not stop solely with his support of the rebuilding effort; from his royal revenues, he also financially supported the Levites and song leaders well after the completion of the wall.

The income of the Levites and song leaders was based solely upon the tithes and offerings of the people. As the people were just coming back from exile, their gifts and tithes were most likely not overly plentiful. King Artaxerxes' additional support provided stability during a time of potential financial volatility. Beyond this financial support, King Artaxerxes also exempted the Levites and singers from tolls, tributes, customs, and taxes of every kind (Ezra 7:24).

The king had no earthly reason to provide this support. Upon completion of the wall and the establishment of a local government, he could have expected tributes to begin flowing back to him. Instead, he continued his financial support. Was it simply a matter of "the enemy of my enemy is my friend"? Nothing indicates this to be the case. For whatever reason, he crossed the boundaries of class and race to support the Israelites.

A robust change management strategy in the corporate world includes identifying and leveraging the support of persons within an organization who are considered "influencers." Getting these people to become early adopters of any upcoming change can critically impact the success rate of the endeavor. Seeking out and leveraging these people is needed for effective ministry as well.

We should never be lulled into thinking that because we want something to happen or believe specific changes are in the best interests of those we lead, people will automatically embrace these changes. We may know an issue inside and out. We may have all the information and data needed to support our direction or choices, but excluding others from involvement in key decisions often lies at the root of a mission's failure.

You need to know those most likely to sway others with their opinions. Not only develop a game plan that includes their involvement and support but one where everyone on your team understands their role. Imagining that we can rely only on ourselves to lead is a mistake.

Our church has two formal bi-yearly congregational meetings with bi-monthly town hall meetings. These town halls allow a time of open communication from our leadership team to our congregants and time for the congregation to provide input back. These meetings are crucial in helping us identify the unlikely supporters and influencers passionate about a particular issue, allowing us to tap into their energy or insight as we move forward.

First Corinthians teaches us the importance of the different members of the body of Christ. "For even as the body is one and yet has many members, and all the members of the body, though they are many, are one body, so also is Christ" (1 Cor. 12:12). This passage explains why each person, even those we may deem not as essential as others, is needed. The verse continues: "On the contrary, it is much truer that the members of the body which seem to be weaker are necessary" (1 Cor. 12:22).

Look amongst those you lead for the influencers. Do not expect them always to be the most powerful or outspoken people. Those who can make the most significant impact often have the softer voices. Do not set out to get others simply to buy into your plans. Rather, engage with these people first through listening. You may begin to see something from an angle not previously considered. Through this intentional engagement, you may even unknowingly gain their support.

SUMMARY

The relational leadership concepts within this chapter explored the dynamics associated with three different types of people that we often encounter in life or ministry. Dealing with others can be one of the more complex areas of leadership. God has placed you in certain relationships. Employing the concepts in this chapter can help you lead these relationships in a way that honors Him.

Our first concept explored working with those who are considered super-volunteers. It is critically important to develop a succession plan to ensure a smooth transition as their time in ministry ends.

The second leadership concept delved into handling those who believe their length of time at church, financial giving, or relationship they have with you would entitle them to more decision-making power or authority than others. Wisdom would help us learn to stand our ground in their presence and against their demands.

Our last concept encouraged us to seek out those who might be unlikely supporters but who can significantly affect the direction of our ministries and leadership. Reaching out, listening to, and engaging the support of these influencers is crucial before charging ahead.

You have unique gifts that can (and should) be blended with others to work toward the goal of serving God together. Jesus says, "And the glory which Thou hast given Me I have given to them; that they may be one, just as We are one" (John 17:22). Unity in Jesus will bridge any gaps.

CONSIDER

Considering those you lead or the ministries in which you are engaged, what involvement have you seen by the three types of people described in this chapter? What would leveraging the leadership concepts in this chapter look like, and what impact could they have?

PRAYER

Holy Spirit, help me be open to letting You work through me. I ask for Your wisdom to see what others can bring to the table. May I never believe that I have all the answers. I need to rely on the giftings You have imparted to others to work out Your purpose. I humbly ask for You to give me eyes to see others for who You have created them to be. Let me be part of building a ministry that, first and foremost, draws others to You. Amen.

~12~

Wholehearted Celebration

And on that day they offered great sacrifices and rejoiced because God had given them great joy, even the women and children rejoiced, so that the joy of Jerusalem was heard from afar (Neh. 12:43).

Something is special about the grand opening of . . . anything! Whether it is a new Costco, the remodel of a local YMCA, the opening of a new school, or even a business under new ownership, a grand opening is a chance to celebrate.

I love to attend openings of new facilities and see the joy of families wandering through rooms with balloons and streamers, food everywhere, and helpful people eager to talk about the new facility or available services. There is hope mixed with excitement and endless possibilities.

I recently attended a ribbon-cutting ceremony for a bridge south of downtown Seattle. I was the project manager early in the project. Although I had not been involved in the final phases, I was familiar with the issues encountered before construction.

I hadn't been onsite in months, and the physical reality of seeing what had previously only been on paper was impressive. The concepts that had been envisioned were even better in real life.

As we walked around the site, I spoke with the construction manager about many of the difficulties we had encountered. Each seemed so distant now. In the excitement of the opening, they no longer seemed important. The structure was a complete success, and it was time for those involved in any project phase to come together and celebrate.

Picking up in Nehemiah 12:27, plans were finally underway for the wall's dedication. As with completing any major capital works project, the ceremony was planned with great care and detail. Men, women, and children of all ages were invited. The wall's completion was marked by momentous joy and excitement, and the second half of Nehemiah 12 is dedicated to details of the grand opening.

We celebrate Jesus' resurrection on Easter, a day marked with praise, joy, and hope. Like attending an open house, there is renewed cause for rejoicing each year as we remember what Jesus has done for us. Jesus' last words, "It is finished" (John 19:30), are a statement of supreme hope as His sacrifice ultimately ended the separation between God and man for all time. In his final act, Jesus accomplished the one thing we could not do, build, or create on our own.

This chapter explores several spiritual leadership concepts associated with the wall's dedication. The first concept is learning to balance a friendship with Jesus with the holiness of God. It is never just one or the other; both always coexist. Our second concept sets us free to celebrate and rejoice in the success God brings our way. The final idea in this chapter explores how our celebration is incomplete unless we include space for giving back to God.

Preparation

A wedding can be one the most significant celebrations we experience in our lifetime. Time of preparation can last upwards of fourteen months, with endless checklists being filled out to make the day perfect. Venues may offer a wedding planner to ensure everything is done when needed, particularly on the day of the event. No detail is left to chance, from a "Save the Date" announcement to the day-after champagne brunch.

The average cost of a wedding in the United States (2020 data by Value Penguin at Lending Tree) is $24,723, although it varies significantly by geographic locale. The average number of attendees is 136. There are statistics for the costs of venues, engagement rings, reception bands, photography, florists, décor, favors, officiants, invitations, and so on. One statistic seems to be missing—premarital counseling.

While people may say that getting married is the most significant decision of their life, the Barna Group states that only about 9 percent of those getting married attend premarital counseling. This is amazing when you consider that marriages for those who participate in premarital counseling are much more likely to be successful. Marriage preparation is not just about logistics and details; premarital counseling is intended to ensure we are in alignment with our future spouse.

The dedication of the wall was a huge event. Much preparation had gone into scripting the details of the day. Yet before any celebrating began, the Israelites first prepared their hearts. "And the priests and the Levites purified themselves; they also purified the people, the gates, and the wall" (Neh. 12:30). Before any celebration, everything that would be part of the ceremony had to be purified before God.

No specifics were given for the purification requirements but based on other ceremonies in the Old Testament, we have a good idea. First, the priests would have washed their clothes to remove any potential uncleanness, with Leviticus 22:1–6 providing additional details for their purification. Next, the people would have undergone a type of purification like in Exodus 19:10–15 where the people washed their garments and sanctified themselves before receiving the Ten Commandments.

Finally, even the walls and gates would have been purified before the ceremony. Most likely, they would sprinkle water and say prayers over each gate and at random places along the top of the wall where the people would walk during the dedication. The preparation was intentional; a deep cleansing was needed before this wall could be considered ready to be consecrated to God.

Remember that every gift or sacrifice given to God was required to be pure and without blemish or mark. Any priest with an imperfection or defect would not be allowed to go near to the altar until purified (Lev. 21:21–23), and any flaw in the offering, the person making the offering, or the offering itself would make that gift profane in God's eyes.

The wall's dedication was not a simple ribbon-cutting ceremony or event, with speeches by dignitaries, after which everyone could return to their daily business. God commissioned this wall, and the dedication was nothing less than a ceremony whereby the wall was given back to God.

This was not just a public works project—Jerusalem was the place chosen by God for His dwelling. God's acceptance of this gift was significant. As a gift, they needed to purify all participants and the wall itself before it would be acceptable to God.

Too often, God can be left entirely out of the equation when something we have been working toward is successful. We may give thanks, but we may not understand the importance of dedicating the success back to God as a gift.

Even our thankfulness should be considered a gift that is intentional and given without blemish. Sometimes, we may need to step back before we idly give a gift of thanks back to God, so we can first confirm our hearts are right with God.

We must never forget that while God desires to be our friend, the relationship is never one of equals. Jesus calls us His friends (John 15:14), and we are adopted as His children (Rom. 8:16; Gal. 4:5–9; Eph. 1:5). But this does not mean we can forget God's holiness. He is continually surrounded by creatures crying, "Holy, Holy, Holy, is the Lord of hosts, the whole earth is full of His glory" (Isa. 6:3).

Jesus being our friend does not negate His holiness. Hebrews 7:26 tell us, "For it was fitting that we should have such a high priest, holy, innocent, undefiled, separated from sinners and exalted above the heavens." Understanding and embracing the righteousness of God is imperative, including the proper understanding of how holiness plays into every gift or thank-you we offer. We should never be glib or trivial with anything we give to Jesus.

An integral component of leading well is modeling a healthy tension between our friendship with God and His holiness. Work to understand the balance between the two and how they coexist. Think through ways to offer praise, thanks, and that will be acceptable to Him, considering His holiness.

Let's Party!

The Russian Orthodox Church is widely recognized as

having been established by the apostle Andrew as he evangelized along the northern coast of the Black Sea. The formalized religion was founded by Saint Vladimir the Great in 988 AD and currently claims over 112 million members worldwide. The services are predominantly classified as "high church" with a strong emphasis on ritual and liturgical practices. They have a formal structure for almost everything within the service, which extends to special vestments worn by the clergy, including a specific order and ceremony for donning these garments.

Worship begins with a processional entry of the clergy accompanied by a cross and candles or banners carried by acolytes (altar attendants). The processional is an elaborate affair with great pomp and often includes the use of icons, bells, incense, and chanting.

My parents visited me when I lived and worked in Alaska early in my engineering career. My father, who had a great interest in participating in the practices of other religions, requested that we go to a Russian Orthodox service. That single service we attended has stayed firmly etched in my mind.

Worship was conducted in a small, dark, incense-filled sanctuary. While we did not understand a single word, we left with a deep connection in worship with the Most Holy God. Our attendance was an unbelievable blessing.

While the processional was relatively small, one only needs to search the images of "orthodox procession" on the internet to see processions celebrating a special event or leading to worship. Thousands of followers appear in these majestic processions.

One time we happened to be in Mexico during Holy Week. We witnessed thousands of people from all walks of life streaming along a dried riverbed in the city on their way to the central cathedral in town.

Close to five thousand people must have attended the reenactment of the crucifixion of Jesus. The streets, sidewalks, and beaches were utterly packed, and celebration was in the air. This strikes me as possibly what the dedication of the wall around Jerusalem would have been like.

The priests, people, and wall were purified, and the people were ready to offer the wall as a gift to God. It was time for the dedication! Carefully orchestrated by Nehemiah, the procession was comprised of two separate "thanksgiving choirs" (Neh. 12:31). Each choir proceeded in opposite directions from a single starting point on the top of the wall.

The leaders and the people followed their respective choirs as they marched along the entire top of the wall, all the way around Jerusalem until they met and blended back into one unified body in the house of God for singing, sacrifices, and celebration. The celebration included everyone, not just the leaders, nobles, or men: "The women and children rejoiced" (Neh. 12:43). The celebration and rejoicing were so exuberant that the joy was "heard from afar" (Neh. 12:43).

The words "encompassed in joy" come to mind when we read this section of Nehemiah. They have reasons to rejoice and celebrate. The people have overcome seemingly insurmountable obstacles and difficulties to rebuild the wall. Thankfulness is in their hearts amidst great revelry and joy.

Depending on the version used, the word "joy" is used approximately 430 times in the Bible, whereas "celebrate" is used fewer than 100 times. The reason is easy to understand.

We are encouraged to be joyful and rejoice always (1 Thess. 5:16), including times of ease, difficulty, and struggle. We are never told that we are to celebrate these times of travail, just to rest in the joy that comes from knowing that God is in control, even under challenging circumstances.

I have a particular relative who enjoys complaining. This person does not just complain about misfortune; there is a constant "Woe is me" attitude, often paired with self-deprecating talk. The words that come out seek affirmation and praise for how much this person endures. There is an unhealthy attachment to celebrating the difficulties of life. That is not how Jesus wants us to celebrate. Instead, we should let our celebration reflect praise for who God is and what He has done.

Psalms 111–113, 117, 135, and 146–150 begin with the phrase, "Praise the Lord!" While the book of Psalms is filled with celebration and praise to God, these ten psalms of celebration have a slightly different focus. They ascribe glory and honor to God. They thank God for His goodness, prosperity, wonderful works, help, Jerusalem's restoration, and exalting of the humble. The mood invoked by these psalms is celebratory: Look at what God has done!

This should be our attitude approaching celebrations. We have ample reason to party for no other reason than because we know God. My brother is big on family events. As nothing seems to be too small for them to celebrate, we often find ourselves being invited to his house for every possible occasion. He takes any excuse to make joyful times in their lives into memorable moments of celebration. We can learn much from this type of example.

Celebrate! Lift praises to God! Your life and ministries should not simply be a series of weekly events to fit into your schedule. Nor should celebrations be constrained only to specific yearly events. Looks for ways to integrate celebrations into your calendar. Times of refreshing (Acts 3:19) are tied to the presence of the Lord. That is reason enough to celebrate!

Tribute

We often associate tribute with affirmations or acclamations spoken about another person. Events such as memorials, anniversaries, awards, weddings, or reunions often include a tribute to one or more persons to honor them.

A tribute typically offers accolades that highlight the accomplishments or praiseworthy characteristics of the one being honored or include giving gifts or tokens of appreciation. A tribute is defined as "acts, statements, or gifts intended to show gratitude, respect, or admiration."

Over the years, the late Queen of England received thousands of gifts. At the Summer Opening of Buckingham Palace in 2017, over 250 gifts were placed on public display. These presents include a Canadian totem pole, a Zambian silver bowl with fruit, Yoruba thrones, and countless crowns and jewels from around the world.

Each tribute presented to Queen Elizabeth was given not only to honor her position as a ruling monarch but provides a glimpse into the precious treasures and culture of the people giving the gift. These prized works of art and gifts are given freely, with no compulsion or expectation of a return gift or favor.

The concept of a tribute dates to ancient times. Rather than being given freely, tributes were typically exacted from a conquered people as a sign of submission or allegiance. Tributes of wealth would be expected to be paid to the more powerful party of an alliance or to finance projects that might benefit both parties. Tributes were centered around political power and submission. Senator William Learned Marcy said in 1832, "To the victor belong the spoils."

Embedded in the concept of a tribute is the assumption that the payment or gift is somehow owed to the other party due to their status, power, or position. Indeed, tributes exist independent of a desire on the giver's part or an appreciation on the receiver's part. A conqueror would not necessarily expect the conquered party to be thankful to give the required tribute.

How often do we think about our offerings as a form of tribute? God is the recipient, whether an offering is given willingly or under compulsion. Nehemiah 12 closes with arranging the tribute collection specified in the law of Moses. Tributes were required to be given to all priests, Levites, singers, and gatekeepers who served God. These offerings were gathered with joy (Neh. 12:44) and included contributions of first fruits and tithes.

Second Corinthians 9:7 says, "Let each one do just as he has purposed in his heart; not grudgingly or under compulsion; for God loves a cheerful giver." God has asked us to bring Him our tithes as a tribute to Him for who He is and what He has done for us.

While our attitude toward giving may not be important when a tribute is given to others, it is vitally significant when we give to God. Deuteronomy 16:17 tells us: "Every man shall give as he is able, according to the blessing of the Lord your God which He has given you." Giving with joy and thankfulness comes as we remember that all we have been given is from God.

Several years ago, it became popular in some church circles to tweak the focus from tithing to giving our "time, talents, and treasures." This gained in popularity so quickly for a variety of reasons. As people became busier and more women started working outside the home, volunteer positions were more difficult to fill.

The idea was to recognize that the role of serving God was not limited to dropping money on the plate each Sunday but also included serving as a volunteer with our time and talents. It was intended to capture more of a person's life in service to God.

Unfortunately, this also became some people's excuse to not give as much financially. Even worse, the attitude shifted to where our giving became more about us and how we could fit more of God into our lives and feel good about our service rather than living solely for Him. Little by little, we moved away from His call to "Follow Me" with all we have and are.

It becomes easy to make excuses for giving Him less, justifying this under the guise of our busyness for Him. While there is certainly nothing wrong with sharing our talents or providing our time in His service, that should never be an excuse to give less financially.

Most leaders cannot begin to count the hours they put in each week. To the extent that God has blessed you with leadership skills, honor Him by not only serving Him wholeheartedly but by never using your service as an excuse to reduce your financial tribute.

In the widow's mite story in Mark 12:41–44, Jesus reminds us that the widow gave "out of her poverty . . . all she had to live on." She kept nothing back for herself. That is a tribute worthy of our King and something we would do well to emulate.

SUMMARY

What joy it would be to hear Jesus say, "Well done, good and faithful servant" (Matt. 25:23) at the culmination of my life's journey. This chapter delved into the deep-seated joy that comes with following through and completing the work God has given us. It may seem counterintuitive to talk about how to lead through joy, yet we are not called to lead only through difficulties. As you celebrate joyful times, the concepts in this chapter are expressly provided to help you do so in a way that honors Jesus.

Our first leadership concept in this chapter focused on the critical understanding we must have of God's holiness when we offer Him our gifts. Purifying our hearts and minds before giving anything to God is a crucial leadership skill.

Secondly, we explored the joy accompanying completing what He has called us to do. We should not miss opportunities for rejoicing and celebrating when we have finished tasks. Look for ways to include a celebration with those who serve with you.

The final leadership concept deepened our understanding that our gifts and offerings are a tribute to our King. Modeling an attitude of giving allows others to understand this concept more than any words we could say. We need to make space for giving back to God what He is due.

CONSIDER

We can easily overfocus on work or ministries without pausing to recognize and celebrate what has been accomplished. Think of ways to celebrate small achievements, being careful to not neglect to prepare your heart to come before your King. How can you make small movements toward all celebrations and gifts being a tribute to God?

PRAYER

Mighty God, I acknowledge Your power and glory. Help me learn the connection between friendship with You and Your holiness. Father, may I walk through life with profound joy for the work You have called me to, with everything I do or accomplish being given back to You as a tribute. I ask for endurance to be able to run the race You have set before me. You are the author and perfector of my faith. May I be faithful to the end. Amen.

❦13❦

Uncompromised Faith

Thus I purified them from everything foreign (Neh. 13:30).

SOCIETAL NORMS STRONGLY IMPACT OUR LIFE. We are faced with unwritten expectations about doing well in school, attending college, getting a good job, getting married, having 2.5 children, and living the American dream. Further pressure is exerted to drive the right car, live in the right neighborhood, wear the right clothes, listen to the right music, be invited to the right parties, and live like everyone else.

My husband and I live in a school district where attending college after high school is the norm. Students graduate with an average of six AP credits and are encouraged to earn college credits during high school. Classes are rigorous, and the pressure on grades is intense. Children with learning disabilities or who are not interested in college are often seen by peers, teachers, or counselors as not trying or unwilling to conform.

But unlike this popular thinking, our success in life is not necessarily tied to our conformance to societal norms. Sometimes we should be willing to walk our own path. If a situation ever presents itself where a question arises of whether we should conform to society or go where Jesus is calling, Jesus should always trump.

In Nehemiah 13, Nehemiah had just returned from time away in King Artaxerxes' court. We do not know the length of his stay in Susa, but upon his return, Nehemiah found that the Israelites' lifestyles had begun to conform to those of the foreigners with whom they lived.

Eliashab, the high priest who rebuilt the Sheep Gate and was therefore presumably present when Ezra read the law of Moses, had taken the room which held contributions for the priests and Levites and converted it into living quarters for Tobiah (Nehemiah's opponent in chapters 2, 4, and 6). He withheld the Levites' allotments, causing them to return to working in their fields to survive. Additionally, and against Nehemiah's specific commands, Jerusalem was now open to commerce on the Sabbath, and the Israelites had begun entering mixed marriages with foreigners.

As the book of Nehemiah ends, Nehemiah again reinstates God's Law. In this chapter, we will explore three spiritual leadership concepts that arise from a life of obedience. The first concept is to understand the importance of living for Jesus, particularly when no one is watching. Secondly, we are reminded of how easy it is for little sins to grow, impacting our relationships with others and God. The last concept focuses on the value of our legacy.

Each section is based on the truth that we must not conform to the lifestyles of those around us. Romans 12:2 (NLT) says, "Don't copy the behavior and customs of this world, but let God transform you into a new person by changing the way you think. Then you will learn to know God's will for you, which is good and pleasing and perfect." We should only conform to the life Jesus calls us to.

When No One Is Looking

For many years I worked in downtown Boston, commuting forty-two miles daily by train. The commute could easily add one and a half hours to my day each way. I quit working during my first pregnancy, but a few months after my son was born, I was asked if I would be willing to return to work part-time. Knowing my lengthy commute, they willingly let me work exclusively from home.

Seven years later, we moved from Boston to Seattle. Microsoft had such a strong presence in Seattle that I naturally assumed I could continue telecommuting. After all, I was still with the same firm. I could not imagine the company having different policies in other locales.

How wrong I was! No one in the Seattle office telecommuted, nor were they the least bit interested in me doing so. This office did not know me or my work ethic. It was a matter of trust, and they did not know me well enough to trust me.

—————

There is an adage that says, "When the cat's away, the mice will play." Posed as a question, "If no one is watching, how will you behave?" Nehemiah had been in Jerusalem for three years before returning to Susa. He had completed the wall, established a local government, reinstituted the practices and laws of his people, and been a steadfast, resolute leader. The governance of the city was going well, and he may have figured it was safe for him to step away for a bit.

This is the classic case of the mice playing while the cat is gone. I wonder what was going through the people's minds when he left. Did they think he would stay in Susa? Would someone else be assigned as the governor, maybe someone who might not be so strict about the law of Moses? For whatever reason, they began wandering from God when he was not there to watch them.

I cannot help but think of this parallel to the ministry of Jesus, which was also an approximately three-year period. For the most part, the men He chose were a ragtag group. He knew that with His leaving, it would be up to them to continue following Him, even when no one was looking. The entire future of Christianity hung in the balance.

How easy it would have been to go back to their old lives. In fact, that is precisely what Simon Peter did: he took several other disciplines and went out fishing (John 21). When Jesus met them there, they renewed and recommitted themselves to a life of following Him at all costs. Never again are we told that Simon Peter questioned his discipleship or struggled with the choice of potentially returning to his former lifestyle. Jesus commanded Peter with the words, "You follow Me!" (John 21:22). And he did.

———

Sometimes I wonder if God sees me. It can be concerning to believe He is watching because if He is, it leads me to question whether He cares. I wonder if my life matters. Sometimes, I feel invisible in the grand scheme of things.

If you have ever felt this way, you are not alone. Trust is a two-way street. It is not just about whether God can trust us with His message of salvation but whether we can trust that God is watching and with us, regardless of whatever we are going through. The question becomes whether we will trust Him, even when we do not feel His presence.

We need to recognize the tension between our spiritual and personal lives. The key to handling this tension is to identify and embrace it. It can be good. Relegating Jesus only to spiritual activities too often leads to compromise. The integration of Jesus into all areas of our lives allows our lives to fully reflect our trust in Him.

For example, a church governance board may decide to handle all business affairs to prevent the pastor from getting bogged down in minutiae, thinking it will allow that pastor to better attend to the congregation's spiritual needs. Yet without integrating a spiritual component into the business side of things, there is a danger of legalism. Operating solely from a business sense can give rise to a perception that we are responsible rather than God. We can forget that He is leading, not us.

He is in our midst, watching. Not in the sense of hoping to find us doing something wrong, but in the sense that we need to realize that our actions, decisions, and direction should always be made in the light of knowing He is present.

Psalm 139:7–12 says, "Where can I go from Thy Spirit? Or where can I flee from Thy presence? If I ascend to heaven, Thou art there; if I make my bed in Sheol, behold, Thou art there. If I take the wings of the dawn, if I dwell in the remotest part of the sea, even there Thy hand will lead me, and Thy right hand will lay hold of me." He is always near, always watching.

When we wonder if He is indeed near, we need only look to Isaiah 41:10: "Do not fear, for I am with you" or Psalm 33:18: "The eye of the Lord is on those who fear Him, on those who hope for His lovingkindness." We can trust Him, which allows us to live in a way that honors Him, even when no one is looking.

A Little Leaven

Many people have tried their hand at making homemade bread. Someone recently gave me some sourdough starter in the hope that I would enjoy baking bread as much as she. She baked daily, and I often saw photos of her freshly baked creations on Facebook. That gracious offer still makes me smile. I am one of those who absolutely loves to make bread—once a year.

Each Christmas, I make delicious cardamom bread from a recipe handed down through our family. "Yearly" is a frequency that suffices. This nerve-racking prospect consumes a full day every year. The most stressful part is wondering if my bread will rise.

One year, I carefully dissolved the yeast in warm milk, added butter, sugar, and salt to the remainder, and then added it to the flour. Although I waited for it to rise for thirty, forty, then fifty minutes, it still had only risen a little in the pan. Was the room too cold? What had I done wrong?

So, I started again, with the same result. It never occurred to me that yeast could expire. Only after buying new yeast did I learn about expiration dates. If the yeast has expired, nothing will cause it to reactivate.

———

The Bible has much to say about yeast (or leaven). Galatians 5:9 states, "A little leaven leavens the whole lump of dough." The book of Nehemiah gives several examples of how sin is like leaven, slowly permeating our lives and causing people to move farther away from the life to which God had called them.

How could it hurt for the Levites to earn their own bread? Why should the government be forced to supply their needs? Didn't it make sense to move Tobiah into the now-empty storeroom? After all, they might as well get some use from that room, particularly since they did not need it for the Levite's supplies anymore.

What about the Sabbath? If they were in the process of creating a great and mighty nation in Jerusalem, wouldn't they need to compete with their neighbors and open their gates for business on the Sabbath? Wouldn't the extra commerce help stimulate the economy, making the people better off?

Finally, were they not called to love their neighbors? Why would that not extend to loving marriages? How could it hurt? If they remained faithful to God, why couldn't their spouse worship their own gods? The people probably never intended the consequences Nehemiah encountered upon his return. After all, it was only a slight compromise here or there. Small concessions that made so much sense!

Contrasting examples of leaven are in the Bible, working both good and evil. First Corinthians 5:6–8 states, "Your boasting is not good. Do you not know that a little leaven leavens the whole lump of dough?" This matches the previous passage from Galatians that said leaven is not good.

However, in Luke 13:20–21, Jesus says, "To what shall I compare the kingdom of God? It is like leaven, which a woman took and hid in three pecks or meal, until it was all leavened." Here Jesus talks about leaven being good.

Leaven in and of itself is neither good nor bad; it depends solely upon how it is used. We must recognize that leaven will work throughout whatever substance it is placed in and then spread throughout. If sin is creeping in, it must be addressed immediately to keep it from spreading. If we have decided to follow Jesus, we must let that decision spread through all our words, deeds, and actions, helping us to think, act, and relate more like Jesus each day.

Numerous Bible studies focus on the "fruit of the Spirit" found in Galatians 5:22-23: "But the fruit of the Spirit is love, joy, peace, patience, kindness, goodness, faithfulness, gentleness, self-control." It is good and right to encourage and exhort each other to let such fruit grow in our lives. If we consider these virtues as leaven, letting each spread allows more and more growth.

We typically consider the corresponding listing of deviant virtues, which occurs just before the fruit of the Spirit, much less frequently; however, it is also an important list. "Now the deeds of the flesh are evident, which are: immorality, impurity, sensuality, idolatry, sorcery, enmities, strife, jealousy, outbursts of anger, disputes, dissensions, factions, envying, drunkenness, carousing and things like these" (Gal. 5:19–21).

Where the fruit of the Spirit includes nine positive traits, this Scripture provides fourteen contaminants we should guard against, and then to be safe adds, "and things like these."

These two passages show that leaven is not limited to specific actions. Attitudes, mindsets, and lifestyles are also in play. Look at the fruit that is in your life and those you lead. What leaven is working? With God's grace, you can determine what kind of leaven you want working through your life.

We can do nothing to make leaven happen. Once started, it works of its own accord, permeating every area of our lives. We only need to be open to the Holy Spirit to work in and through our lives.

What Is Your Legacy?

In the mid-eighties, several new bridges were designed and constructed on I-25 outside downtown Denver, Colorado. As the lead designer for several of these bridges, and with this being my first major bridge project, I took quite a few photos of the new bridges before returning to Seattle. Years later, as we drove through Denver on a cross-country trek from Boston to Seattle, I tracked down one of these bridges to show my then five- and seven-year-old children.

What a shock! I thought we had the wrong place. The previously pristine, new sidewalks were cracked and buckled, the embankments were overgrown, the bridge bearings no longer functioned, and the overall structure simply looked ... well ... old. My children, suitably unimpressed, asked, "Is this it?" In my mind, I still saw the glistening new bridge I had left years before. The reality was completely different.

The shocking moment reminded me that nothing we do in our time on earth will remain. Everything is subject to the ravages of time. The Psalms remind us of the fleeting nature of our time on earth. "Man is like a mere breath; his days are like a passing shadow" (Ps. 144:4). We long for something that will remain after we are gone. We long to leave a legacy.

Each time that Nehemiah righted one of the wrongs he discovered upon his return to Jerusalem, he pled for God to "remember him." These were not the only times he asked this of God. In Nehemiah 5:19, he asked God to remember him after righting the injustices his people were facing. Again, in Nehemiah 6:14, after standing against personal attacks meant to derail the wall, he asked God to remember what his enemies had done to him.

Nehemiah specifically asked for a legacy that was not tied to the world. He did not consider the rebuilt wall to be a worthy one. Nehemiah knew that someday even this massive undertaking would be gone. His inheritance lay in the service he gave to God. His only desire was for God to know and honor his undivided heart for Him. One unfailing characteristic of Nehemiah's life throughout this book is his unwavering faith in God and willingness to allow God to use him.

Nehemiah's request highlights a focus on how, through seemingly impossible odds, his faith remained intact. His faith was the driver of all he did, and it sustained him through every trial he encountered. Others had fallen away, but he remained steadfast.

A word that defines this type of faith is endurance, which means "staying power in difficult or unpleasant situations." These words do not come easily. Here are a few verses to ponder:

The testing of your faith produces endurance (James 1:3).

Let us also lay aside every encumbrance, and the sin which so easily entangles us, and let us run with endurance the race that is set before us (Heb.12:1).

By your endurance you will gain your lives (Luke 21:19).

These verses remind us that we will be tested and enticed by sin. Yet Jesus' words of assurance in Luke promise a reward for our endurance—life itself. God will remember us not for our personal accomplishments but for our perseverance as we serve God with all we have through both easy and challenging times. That is our legacy.

———

A man in our church exemplified a life of endurance. He was often asked to serve on committees and held various leadership positions. A well-respected professional, he was also a little intimidating and often came across as condescending.

He died after a long, debilitating battle with Parkinson's. The congregation watched as he slowly lost mobility and succumbed to this dreadful disease. But what happened to him during his illness was incredible. The less he was physically able to do, the softer his heart became. Less mobility resulted in a flood of love and humility in his spirit.

During an interview about a year before his death, he spoke of earnestly praying for healing. As the disease progressed and his physical symptoms became more and more acute, he realized that he had received the healing for which he had prayed. It just did not come in the way he expected. He had been healed—from himself.

His testimony was one of the most powerful things I have ever heard. His faith in God, unwavering to the end, brought him freedom of spirit that might never have happened otherwise. His legacy was in the lives he touched, his endurance, and his witness for Jesus to the end.

Our personal legacy may not match what we want it to be. We may believe our heritage should be based on what we have done. But a legacy is not something we can control or create—it is something people recognize once we are gone. During your life, you may find yourself serving God with different groups of people. Each of these groups will remember you differently. The heart you served with will be remembered more than anything else. That is what will cause your legacy to be created.

SUMMARY

In his book entitled *The Cost of Discipleship*, Dietrich Bonhoeffer states, "The cost of discipleship never consists of this or that specific action; it is always a decision, either for or against Christ" (p226). This powerful statement lends itself well as the lens through which we can view this chapter on obedience.

Spiritual leadership first requires that we do not conform to society around us but to Jesus. This guiding leadership principle must be embraced and lived out before all else. As a leader, set an example for others to follow using the leadership concepts in this chapter as a guide.

Our first concept is understanding who we are, how we act, and what we do when no one is looking must be bound by our decision to follow Jesus. We choose to live for Jesus regardless of who is watching.

The second concept we explored was understanding that each decision we make will act as leaven in our lives. Little sins will grow until our very faith is compromised. Conversely, the leaven of small decisions for Jesus will grow into an abundant, life-giving faith.

Our last leadership concept spoke to the truth that our legacy is not about what we have done but who we are when we serve. Our legacy before God will be based on what is in our hearts.

CONSIDER

As we close, consider what elements you expect to see in a life of "uncompromised faith." Tie each of the three spiritual leadership concepts in this chapter to that definition. Working through each element you have selected, can you describe the role obedience plays?

PRAYER

Holy Lord God, help me see the world as You see it so that I do not question whether what I do is conforming to the world or to You. I pray that Your love will become a leaven in my life, spreading throughout my whole being. In humility, I ask that You remember me not for what I have done but only for my love for You. May my heart always be turned toward You, with the strength to choose You in every situation. Amen.

Conclusion

We have completed our journey through the book of Nehemiah. We have reached the end of our path together. This conclusion will be our return journey, where we walk along the same pathway we just traveled, looking at it one last time to capture and embrace the ideas and concepts God intended.

Through the thirteen chapters in Nehemiah, separate seemingly incongruent leadership concepts are woven into a single unit that merges into one overall arching theme: every person is a leader exactly where they are.

Each chapter focused on one overriding leadership skill, supported by several underlying concepts in each chapter that worked together to cultivate that skill. Along the way, we have learned the following:

- Respond to crisis through prayer.
- Strategic planning requires listening.
- Structured responsibilities set boundaries.
- External assaults require protection.
- Inner turmoil exposes vulnerability.
- Personal attacks keep us persevering.
- New beginnings start with waiting.
- God's Word is our basis for study.
- Mighty deeds establish honor.
- Future focus releases freedom.
- Understanding others is part of service.
- Wholehearted celebration delights in joy.
- Uncompromised faith requires obedience.

One word that encompasses the entirety of these leadership skills is faith. Faith in the Lord God is woven throughout each chapter of this book. From the beginning chapter to the last words, the story of Nehemiah is one of faith.

God is the first person Nehemiah goes to when trouble comes, and no action is taken before consulting with Him. Nehemiah's faith in God is at the center stage through every issue, while organizing his people, setting up a new government, and planning and executing this great public works project. He is not swayed by bribery, uprising, or even when he is gone from Jerusalem. He ensures his people know the law of God and then holds them accountable.

If we take away nothing else from this book than that faith is the basis for all leadership, what a difference we could make! It is not our job to convert people. It is God Himself, and only He, who can draw people to Jesus. Our job is to point the way and allow them to meet Jesus. That is the ultimate goal of leadership.

First Corinthians 3:7 says, "So neither the one who plants nor the one who waters is anything, but only God, who makes things grow." We are called to live by His Word, to love others like Jesus, and to leave the results to God.

Make no mistake. It is our job to hold others accountable for what they know. We are called to know and live by God's Word. As leaders, we cannot shirk the responsibility of guiding and shepherding others. What if, like Nehemiah, we took the responsibility upon ourselves to be sure everyone in our circles of influence knew Him and held them accountable to live righteously before Him? It is not child's play to lead like Nehemiah, with faith coming before all.

At no point does Nehemiah fight or rail against God for

any circumstances or situations in which he finds himself. His faith is woven into his life and sustains him throughout. This faith is what allows God to work mightily through Nehemiah. Rest assured that God will use you as you open yourself more and more to Jesus and allow your faith to grow. You need only be open to it and to Him.

Each of the thirteen chapters in this book provides an essential aspect of leadership. I pray your perception and understanding of your role as a leader have been awakened through this book, and that it gives concepts that build these skills in your life. I intended to develop and expose the idea that you are already a leader! Do you believe that? Embracing and living into these concepts and growing in your faith will continue to allow the leader within you to be further exposed. The challenge is to expand your perception to include yourself as a leader, where God has placed you, and then let Him work.

Appendix - Study Questions

Chapter 1: Respond to Crisis

- Describe yourself. Note what adjectives you use. Is your relationship with Jesus central to that identity?
- Name several sins you are aware of in society or your local community, whether they have personally touched your life or not. What place do you allow grief or confession to have when you consider them? What role, if any, should they play in your response?
- Describe a difficult situation you have encountered. What was your initial response? If you did not fast and pray before acting, how might those elements have changed your answer?
- Describe several promises God has made. Spend time focusing on His provision. Does focusing on how He supplied in the past build an expectation for future action? What if He doesn't act as you hope?

Chapter 2: Strategic Planning

- Do you tend to procrastinate? What situations have you encountered that have led to procrastination? What techniques can you rely on to help you move past procrastination?
- Have you ever acted as a Lone Ranger rather than seeking help from others? Identify your support networks and the influencers within each. Which relationships have you cultivated to be able to activate support when needed?
- Think of a time when you acted on the information at hand, only to discover later that you did not have all the facts. What was your immediate response? Did repentance and confession play a role in the resolution?
- When did you last "rally the troops" to engage others to work toward a common goal? Did you utilize any of the principles included in this chapter? If not, would your results have been different? What ideas would you add?

Chapter 3: Structured Responsibilities

- Think of a group that has a defined organizational structure. Does every team member know their role and the limits of that role? Is the organizational structure ever challenged or refined? What benefit can there be in doing so?
- Can you identify the last situation in which you were involved where a "divide and conquer" approach was used? What was the outcome? If not used, how might the result have changed if this tactic had been tried?
- God can use the unlikeliest people in the most unusual situations for His glory. And yet we often ask the same people over and over to help. How vast is your network of people who can be called upon when needed? How can you broaden that pool to allow an all-hands-on-deck approach in times of crisis?
- Think of a time when you doubted someone's intent. Did you give that person the benefit of the doubt? If so, how did it change their motivation or outcome? If not, what could you do differently next time?

Chapter 4: External Assaults

- Have you ever been mocked for your faith? Are you willing to take a stand as a Christian, even if labeled a fanatic? What is one tangible step you can take to support those elsewhere who are experiencing physical danger as a Christian?
- Can you give an example of a time that you rallied around someone? What made that rally point successful, and what did you learn that can be applied to other situations? Is Jesus your rallying point? How so?
- Do you have one overriding missional priority in your life, or do you regularly question God's plans and calling on your life? Do you have a singularity of focus, or are you easily swayed by the next culturally relevant topic? How can you regain a single-minded focus?
- Can you identify recent changes in your life or the life of your church

that might spark a spiritual or physical attack? Have these changes drawn you closer to Jesus? What role can you play in protecting against such an assault?

Chapter 5: Internal Turmoil

- Did you spend time praying for insight into your motivation at the start of this chapter? If not, do so now. What drives you? What has caused you to be where you are currently in life?
- As you prepare for your next activity, put away your to-do list and speak to others with no other motive than to listen. What are others saying? Seek out several people you have not talked to recently or who may not be in your current circle of influence and start a conversation.
- Do people come to you when they are in turmoil? Can you identify one or two things others say isn't fair (in any arena of your life)? If so, how can you begin conversations that will lead to a resolution?
- What did you want to do when you grew up? How does that differ from who you wanted to be? Can you separate these questions? Would others say humility characterizes your life and lifestyle choices? If not, are you willing to ask God to humble you? What holds you back?

Chapter 6: Personal Attacks

- In areas where you have felt personally attacked, can you identify the root cause or causes? If so, delineate steps you can take to address each root cause. If there are multiple causes, address each in turn.
- Have rumors ever been spread about you? How did you respond? What tools do you have to address them? The next time you hear gossip, what will be your response?
- Do you know what God's call is for your life? Spend time discerning and confirming that call, including being willing to move into a different role. How will you know when it is time to step aside? Are you open to that?

- Have you ever been betrayed? What was your response? Outline steps you could take to rebuild trust with the person who betrayed you. Are you willing to do so?

Chapter 7: New Beginnings

- Have you ever said, "Then God put it into my heart to ..."? How did you respond to that direction? If you have never heard that, spend time resting with Jesus until you can hear Him speak to your heart.
- Can you describe a time when you wondered, What now? How did you move forward? How did that work? Did you wait clearly on God's direction? If not, spend some time journaling how you might have done things differently.
- Name all the groups in which you have a membership. How do these groups differ? Do some provide a deeper sense of belonging? What creates that difference?
- Have you ever been involved in a merger? If it went well, was an integration team involved? If it didn't, what could have been done differently? Either way, apply those lessons to how you would integrate newcomers into your current groups. Are you willing to let them be grafted in, even at the expense of how things are currently done?

Chapter 8: God's Word

- Do you have a living faith in Jesus Christ, or are you a Christian only in name? How would others characterize your faith, and what fruit are you bearing in your life?
- Have you ever been so immersed in God's Word that you cannot put it down? How much time do you spend reading the Bible versus other books, regardless of whether they are a Christian genre? Identify and then cultivate several ways to deepen your study of the Bible.
- Describe how your church provides opportunities for you to grow in your faith. Does a small group meet after the service to discuss the sermon? In what other groups are you engaged? How is studying and growing in Jesus a part of those groups?

- Read and meditate on Psalm 51. When was the last time you openly repented, claiming the blood of Jesus over your sins? Even now, name your sins, allow yourself to grieve and repent, and then claim victory in Jesus' name.

Chapter 9: Mighty Deeds

- Consider the practice of "stones of remembrance." How might this application help you recall God's actions in your life when you do not feel Him near? Is there somewhere visible where you can place your stones?
- How have you seen God work in your story? What are three to five mighty acts God has done in the last year? Commit to making this a quarterly or semi-annual practice with those you lead.
- Do you see either boomerang or yo-yo tendencies in any groups or people you lead? Do emotional decisions carry the day? How can you move decisions to a cognitive level rather than an emotional one? If a course correction is needed, take action.
- Do you like bargains? When was the last time you bargained with God, and what was your attitude when petitioning Him? Explain how and why we are entitled to plead with God.

Chapter 10: Future Focused

- Think about the planning you do before you take a trip. Does that mimic the planning you do before a big decision or change? How does it differ? What elements of trip planning might you want to add?
- Have you ever made a vow or an oath? Think through the obligations associated with each. How would you explain the difference to someone between the oath taken by the Israelites and the freedom offered by Jesus? When is it appropriate to use an oath?
- Do you tithe? Is money talked about freely in your church? Who is involved in shaping your ministry focus? Craft a conversation with those you mentor or lead about healthy giving.
- Explain the difference between a server and a servant (or bond-slave).

Are you more willing to give when it is done out of gratitude or when you are required to do so? How do you model servanthood to those you lead?

Chapter 11: Understand Others

- What have you given up following Jesus? Think of your life before you knew Jesus. Compare that to how you are living now. What is no longer part of your life? What do you still need to surrender to Jesus?
- Have you considered formal succession plans for those who serve with you? How can you walk alongside volunteers who are unsure how to identify and train others to take their place?
- Can you identify any of the "Who's Who" within your social circles or ministries? Think about a time when they exerted power to force an action or decision. What are ways you could counter that in the future?
- Similarly, identify the influencers within your ministry. When was the last time you engaged them for input before enacting a plan? How can they be more fully integrated into upcoming decisions?

Chapter 12: Wholehearted Celebration

- Have you ever been to an opening ceremony of a building or business? Can you relate to the excitement brought about by such an event? Describe ways to bring that same excitement to a ministry or team upon completing each task or goal.
- Fill in the blank: "God is _____." For you, where does His holiness stand in relation to His friendship? When you give Him a gift, write down verses on God's holiness (a concordance can help) and journal your thoughts on the intersection of friendship and holiness.
- Write out your definition of joy. What brings you joy? How do happiness and joy differ? Do you include God in your celebrations? How and what do you celebrate?
- Does splitting a tribute to God into giving of time, talent, and treasure impact your ability to ensure tithing is kept in its proper context as a

tribute to our King? Has the focus on the importance of offering our money to God been diluted? How can it be refreshed?

Chapter 13: Uncompromised Faith

- Have you ever been tempted to conform to societal norms? Describe both the ways you sought to fit in and how you might apply Romans 12:2 in resisting the urge to be like everyone else.
- Are you steadfast in your walk with Jesus, or is it easy to cut corners and justify those actions when no one is looking? Do you have someone who can help hold you accountable for both small and big things? If not, pray about who that could be.
- How do you deal with sin? Can you identify anything that has crept in that interferes with the ministry to which God has called you? What would it look like to focus on embracing good leaven? How can you lead others into that?
- Write one of the following verses on a notecard and commit it to memory: James 1:2–4, Hebrews 12:1–2; Luke 21:19. Journal about what you would like your legacy to be and what you are doing to bring that into being.

About the Author

BARBARA MOFFAT is a Vice President and Market Leader for a consulting engineering firm where she captures new projects and market share while engaging in strategic planning and leadership development. Barbara brings a voice of experience that encompasses a wide range of leadership styles and situations.

CPSIA information can be obtained
at www.ICGtesting.com
Printed in the USA
JSHW042240231122
33226JS00010B/11